THEOLOGICAL INCORRECTNESS

THEOLOGICAL INCORRECTNESS

Why Religious People Believe What They Shouldn't

D. Jason Slone

OXFORD
UNIVERSITY PRESS
2004

OXFORD
UNIVERSITY PRESS

Oxford   New York
Auckland   Bangkok   Buenos Aires   Cape Town   Chennai
Dar es Salaam   Delhi   Hong Kong   Istanbul   Karachi   Kolkata
Kuala Lumpur   Madrid   Melbourne   Mexico City   Mumbai   Nairobi
São Paulo   Shanghai   Taipei   Tokyo   Toronto

Library of Congress Cataloging-in-Publication Data
Slone, D. Jason.
Theological incorrectness : why religious people believe what they
shouldn't / D. Jason Slone.
p.   cm.
Inlcudes bibliographical references and index.
ISBN 0-19-516926-3
1. Psychology, Religious. 2. Cognitive consistency—Religious
aspects. I. Title.
BL53 .S575 2004
200'.1'9—dc21   2003007588

1 3 5 7 9 8 6 4 2

Printed in the United States of America
on acid-free paper

To Brooke

PREFACE

Two facts fascinate me about religion. First, there is more than one religion in the world. That's a strange fact, given that each religion is supposed to be *true*. Second, religious beliefs are incomplete. Since people rarely (if ever) actually get to talk with god(s), believers have to guess about quite a lot—how we originated, who/what God is, what God wants from us, what life is all about, how humans ought to live, why bad things happen to good people and good things happen to bad people, and so on. This, too, is a strange fact, given that religions are supposed to provide *absolute* truth.

It wasn't until I read Justin Barrett's (1999) work on "theological correctness" that I began to piece together an answer to these questions, and many others. His work showed me that the answer was in my head all along. More accurately, the answer was in all of our heads—the answer to these puzzles is to be found in the workings of the human mind. This is the insight the cognitive sciences have to offer students of religion: religion is the way it is because the mind is the way it is.

Though Barrett's work linked the human cognitive capacity for multiple levels of representation with theological belief, I realized that the same body of research could explain the central problems I lump together in this book as "theological incorrectness," or why religious people believe what they shouldn't. Religious people believe what they shouldn't because, the psychological research shows, people think lots of things they shouldn't in general. The human mind is a limited-capacity information processor and therefore, though effective for solving most of the tasks involved in everyday thinking, prone to reasoning errors. Since religion is a product of ordinary cognition, religious people are prone to religious reasoning errors—at least when compared against official theological doctrines.

The insight that religious belief and its corresponding behaviors are explainable at the level of cognition confirmed my sense that advances in the understanding of "cultural" phenomena—including not just religion but also music, art, language, sexual attraction, altruistic virtue, in-group coalitionism, out-group-directed violence, and so on—are going to be made through interdisciplinary research that connects research about culture with research about cognition. Understanding religious belief requires scholarly engagement at multiple levels of analysis; being interdisciplinary, the cognitive science of religion allow scholars to bring together research from otherwise disparate fields like comparative religion, philosophy, anthropology, psychology, and evolutionary biology toward a full account of the origins and functions of religious belief and action. In this regard, this book addresses only one particular feature of religion, but it is a broader plea for greater infusion of the sciences into the humanities. This book is my small contribution to E. O. Wilson's (1998) call for "consilience."

The originality of this book is in its application of new explanatory theories of religious behavior to compelling problems in the study of religion: Is Buddhism really like all the other religions? Why is divine sovereignty a difficult concept to employ in religious thinking? Why are luck beliefs so widespread? Just as important, however, this book provides a survey of the paradigmatic theories in the study of religion broadly and the cognitive science of religion specifically. The book is designed not just to explain theological incorrectness but also to show how theoretical assumptions about human behavior inform scholarly accounts of religion.

As such, I must acknowledge those individuals who have contributed to my theoretical approach to the study of religion. First and foremost, I must acknowledge the profound influence of Tom Lawson on my understanding of religion. Were it not for his pioneering scholarly work and his personal intellectual guidance, this book would not have developed as it has. Lawson's published work has shown conclusively that a cognitive science of religion is not only possible but in fact desirable, and, just as important, his private dialogues with students and colleagues have convinced a new generation of scholars that the cognitive sciences provide the best methods we have (currently) for understanding religious behavior.

Second, I must acknowledge the work of a cadre of scholars in the field from whom I have also benefited greatly. In addition to Tom Lawson, I am indebted to Justin Barrett, Jesse Bering, Pascal Boyer, Stewart Guthrie, Deb Kelemen, Brian Malley, Luther Martin, Robert McCauley, Joel Mort, Todd Tremlin, and Harvey Whitehouse for their insights into the cognitive science of religion. Though the number of scholars working in the field is growing each day, I have particular debts to these individuals.

Third, I would like to acknowledge those individuals who read, reviewed, and commented on the manuscript. In particular I would like to thank Justin Barrett, Scott Johnson, Tom Lawson, Tim Light, Todd Tremlin, Harvey Whitehouse, and Brian Wilson for their constructive criticisms and helpful suggestions.

Fourth, professional work would go undone were it not for those people in my relationship network who give me the space and the means to think and write. In this regard, I must thank my wife, Brooke, for her unwavering love, support, and encouragement. Next, I must thank Larry and Irene Appleby; Ed, Kim, and Amber Hensley; Betty Bowman; Richard and Pauline Schiffer; and the many other important people in my family for giving me a firm foundation from which to grow. I would also like to thank Scott, Marjorie, and Matt Johnson for their support and assistance— not the least of which has been the "Johnson Family Scholarship" fund that provided the much-needed and much-appreciated freedom to pursue advanced intellectual endeavors. Thank you all.

Finally, I must thank the staff at Oxford University Press for their work on the publication of this book. I must thank Cynthia Read for giving this manuscript a chance, and for leading me by the hand through the process of publication. Also, I thank Theo Calderara for his help with the publication process. Your professionalism and expertise are greatly appreciated.

Though many people helped with the production of this book, all mistakes are my own.

CONTENTS

THEOLOGICAL INCORRECTNESS

Is God a Notre Dame Football Fan?

As a resident of the state of Ohio, "God talk" is all around me. Being near the Bible Belt, I commonly hear God's name invoked as an explanation for all sorts of puzzles and problems in life. Political theory is simple: "God helps those who help themselves." Deviant behavior is explained: "It is in our nature to sin." The link between economic well-being and morality is implanted in young children: "Be good, or Santa Claus won't bring you what you want for Christmas."

Furthermore, God is of critical importance when it comes to an aspect of life that matters greatly to Midwesterners—sports, and football in particular. Canton, Ohio, every Ohioan proudly knows, is the birthplace of modern American football. And so surely, I have been told, God is a football fan. After all, Ohio is a God-fearing state.

So you can imagine the angst with which Ohioans endure each and every football season, rooting for their favorite high school, college, and professional teams. A good number of folks in Ohio spend their fall weekends in intense prayer calling on God to help their team win. But the prayers often go unanswered. Ohio teams rarely win championships (the recent Ohio State football national championship was a welcome exception). Over the years, this fact can wear on a person. Not only is it maddening, it can become a theological crisis. Where is God when we need Him most—during the playoffs?!

During a conversation I once had with a Catholic friend ("Catholic by birth and by choice," he would say) he explained the phenomenon quite simply: "Ohio teams usually don't win it all because God is a Notre Dame fan." In one fell swoop, he explained the enigmatic silence with which many Ohioans' prayers are usually answered. But was my friend correct? Is God a Notre Dame football fan?

This book takes as its point of departure Justin Barrett's (1999) notion of "theological correctness." Barrett's research showed that while religious believers produce theologically correct ideas in situations that allow them the time and space to reflect systematically on their beliefs, the same people can stray from those theological beliefs under situational pressures that require them to solve conceptual problems rapidly. Theological incorrectness is the logical extension of that phenomenon—why is it that people believe and do what they *shouldn't*? I don't mean, of course, why do people believe things with which I don't agree? I mean why do people believe things they shouldn't according to the tenets of their own beliefs? Why do religious people kill? Why do religious people philander? Why do Bible believers eat cheeseburgers when the rules in Leviticus say to not mix beef and dairy? Why are religious people racist? Why do religious people pray to win wars? And why do religious people pray to win football games (if God is at all like Christian theologians claim, then certainly he must not care about American football, let alone favor one person's team over another)?

Why is this problem important? It is important because, for one, it teaches us the lesson that theology doesn't determine people's actual thoughts and behaviors. In fact, the ideas that one learns in one's given culture, such as theological ideas, play only a partial role in what people actually think and do. This book offers an explanation for how and why. As I will show, the sorts of ideas we label "religious" are employed only in certain situations, not all the time. As such, culture "nurtures" us less than we tend to think. "Cultural" ideas have causal powers only insofar as ideas are cognitive representations and cognitive representations, because they have physical properties, cause behavior (Barkow, Cosmides, & Tooby 1992; Dennett 1984, 1987; Lakoff & Johnson 1999). This fact should signal the end of the nature/nurture debate because the two are inextricably linked (Pinker 2002). Just keep in mind that terms like "theology," "religion," and "culture" are terms of convenience describing collections of ideas found in people's heads (Sperber 1996).

The book itself is divided into seven chapters. Chapters 1 and 2 explore the ways scholars of religion have thought about religion in the past, concerning the causes of its existence, the role of its functions, and the consequences of its power. Those two chapters review the history of the academic study of religion for the purpose of identifying its common assumptions and its mistakes in thinking about religion. Chapter 3 then explores the cognitive science of religion. I show that the cognitive science of religion provides the best means for understanding religious behavior because it explains religious behavior by situating it in the context of the cognitive origins of human behavior in general. Religion, in all its complexity, is but a natural by-product of our ordinary cognition.

Chapters 4 through 6 employ discoveries about human behavior from the cognitive sciences to explain some recurring and enigmatic case studies from world religions. Specifically, chapter 4 explains one of the oldest problems for scholars of religion—that of "the Buddhist question." Religion is centrally about dealings with postulated superhuman agents, yet Theravada Buddhism is purportedly atheistic. Therefore some scholars familiar with Buddhism have argued that religion cannot be defined as the belief in deities. However, this argument is based on a specious account of Theravada Buddhism, and because Buddhists are capable of theological incorrectness (or "Buddhalogical incorrectness"), they might say that they don't worship the Buddha yet treat him as a superhuman agent, especially in rituals.

Chapter 5 explores the tension in Protestant Christian thought between divine sovereignty and free will. Specifically, I explore this tension as it was played out in the transformation of the English colonies (later the United States of America) from a Puritanical Calvinist society based on the doctrine of absolute divine sovereignty (and thus "predestination") to an Arminianist society based on the combined belief in divine sovereignty and in free will. I provide an epidemiological framework for understanding the spread of Arminianist ideas during the periods of evangelical revival known as "The Great Awakenings." I draw on recent work in cognitive psychology that suggests absolute divine sovereignty is a maximally counterintuitive concept and therefore inherently unstable because of its cognitive burden. Simply put, if God controls everything, then humans control nothing—and that is hard to believe.

Chapter 6 explores the widespread belief in luck. When I say widespread, I mean just that. Scholars have yet to find a culture whose members don't represent some of life's events as lucky or unlucky (or fortunate/unfortunate). Luck is truly a cross-culturally recurring representation. Yet luck is in direct violation of learned theology (all theologies, as far as I can tell). Luck implies that events are beyond our control, and such a notion directly contradicts the very heart of religion—that superhuman agents control events in the world and are responsive to human petitions. Logically, religious people ought never to attribute life's events to luck, but evidence disconfirms this deduction. And if simultaneously holding divergent beliefs in deities and in luck were not perplexing enough, people often perform rituals that are designed to bring about good luck (or bad luck for an enemy) despite the tacit notion that in luck all of life's events are beyond human control.

The book's conclusion then provides some brief reflections on how we might respond to the ubiquity and tenacity of theological incorrectness. Some people feel that it is an impediment to personal and social progress, given our propensities toward violence, racism, sexism, and exploitation and our widespread scientific illiteracy. Imagine if Nancy Reagan's astrological beliefs had influenced her husband to drop the bomb on some unsuspecting Third World nation. Consider that religious violence is believed by the actors—contrary to most theological injunctions—to be divinely sanctioned. Other people, however, suggest that because religion is natural, theological incorrectness is inevitable. Thus, as communist leaders have found, popular religious beliefs (i.e., dangerous beliefs in the eyes of the communist party leaders) cannot be completely rooted out, no matter how much some would like them to be. A third possibility is that while theological incorrectness is natural, common, and cross-cultural, it is certainly not inevitable. Formal education can minimize the less desirable effects of such religious behavior in the world, and that is worth the effort.

CHAPTER ONE

RELIGION IS FOR DUMMIES
AND ROMANTICS

There is an old joke about religion that never bombs, regardless of audience. It goes like this: "If you ask two people of the same religion one question, you'll get three answers." You can tell this joke to Jews, to Buddhists, to Muslims, to Wiccans, to Christians, to whomever, and chances are that they'll respond, with a slight smile, "That's true."

But why is it true, and why is it true for seemingly everyone? If religions teach people what to think about the world, and what they teach is supposed to be true, then why don't their adherents listen very well (a fact that is known all too well by clergy)? To be frank, why do people invent their own versions of religion in whatever ways that seem to suit their fancies? If religion provides people with answers to their questions of ultimate concern, then why are there so many different, competing, contradictory versions of it, even within one single religion?

The joke is funny because, like all jokes, it points out the ridiculous. Two people belonging to the same religion yet having different beliefs is ridiculous if you consider the truth-claims made by the theological contents of religious systems. Yet, though its occurrence at all is ridiculous, what is most interesting is that it occurs just about everywhere; theological incorrectness recurs across cultures.

Most of us are well aware of the existence of theological incorrectness. We might simply dismiss it as an unfortunate but harmless bit of folk religion. In fact, because it is so common most people don't consider it to be weird at all. Upon second glance, however, theological incorrectness challenges every bit of conventional wisdom, and a great deal of the scholarship, that we have about what religion is and how it works. As the joke suggests, and plenty of other evidence confirms, we do not simply learn religion from our culture or society. Rather, we actively generate and transform religious ideas. We might even say, with fashionable jargon from the humanities, that religion is performative.

Religion is performative in three ways: (1) we generate religious representations in our minds (an internal performance); (2) we communicate (in stories, rituals, etc.) some of those representations publicly; and (3) the latter process results in a transformation of religious ideas—sometimes slight, other times considerable—because when others see and hear (i.e., "experience") those representations, they internalize them. The internalization of public representations starts the whole process over again. This is how cultural ideas spread (Sperber 1996).

Though common, the generation and transformation of religious representations by individuals is not always harmless. Consider religious violence. The terrorists who hijacked four jet planes and crashed three of them into the World Trade Center and the U.S. Pentagon on September 11, 2001, killing thousands of innocent global citizens, professed to be Muslims, probably shouting "Alla'u'akbhar" ("God is great!") at the moment of impact. Afterward, many asked how could it be that the religion of Islam justified (read "caused") such violence? Or, given that Islam is a "religion of peace," how could these particular individuals twist their religion's teachings to such horrific ends? Religion, we assume, isn't supposed to work that way. So why does it?

These questions, which millions asked instinctively after September 11, are the right kinds of questions to be asking about the role of religion in our world. But these questions require scientific answers, for ironically the best answers come from neither the religions themselves nor from simple folk psychology (the natural way humans "theorize" about each other's intentions, beliefs, and desires). "Insider" religious answers don't suffice in this case, for obvious reasons: religious answers to questions about religious behavior tend to reflect the beliefs of the person answering the question more than the actual cause(s) of the behavior. Yet folk psychology doesn't get us very far either, because we cannot simply presume that we know instinctively why people do what they do no matter how emotionally satisfying that may be, because humans are often generally unaware of the reasons for their thoughts and actions in the first place. This point was made poignantly by the comedian Bill Cosby, whose children, he claimed, had "brain damage" because whenever he caught them misbehaving and asked them why they did what they did, they would invariably respond, "I don't know!" In most cases, our thoughts and actions simply make sense at the time.

Furthermore, there are other limitations in using folk psychology to understand why religious people think what they think and do what they do that create real problems for students of human behavior because ideas that make sense to some can be nonsense to others. As the old saying goes, one person's garbage is another's treasure. This is commonly the case with studying *someone else's* religion. What other people think and do often seems to be nonsense to us, while our own behavior seems to be perfectly reasonable to us (but to others . . . ?!).

To account for why people do what they do and think what they think, we are better off employing a scientific method because neither the insider's views nor folk psychology will work. Science proves to be much more useful because it reaches "below the surface," so to speak. It does not settle for appearances. Little if anything, for scientists, is obvious. One grand lesson we have learned over the years is that the world isn't necessarily the way it appears to be. Human perceptions are prone to false beliefs. For example, the Earth is not flat and the sun does not move around the Earth, despite our seeing both of those "facts" day after day. Or, despite our seeing obvious in-group human differences like skin color, hair type, languages spoken, and so on, genetics is revealing that we have much more in common than those appearances suggest. And so it shall prove that a scientific study of religious behavior reveals that there are natural causes of behavior that can explain some of the most puzzling aspects of religion in our world (including the very existence of religion itself).

One thing that becomes clear when we begin to apply the science of human behavior to religion is that religious behavior is constrained by the cognitive mechanisms involved in everyday nonreligious behavior. We often think of religion as different, as a special feature of human life. In fact, it is actually dependent on very basic, not-so-special (in the religious sense) mechanisms—namely the cognitive organs in the human brain. Let me provide an example, one that addresses the problem of theological incorrectness just described. When people make what psychologist Justin Barrett has called "online" (i.e., rapid, tacitly informed, cognitively constrained, prereflective) representations, they often employ abductive, not deductive, processes of reasoning. Deductive reasoning involves starting with a general principle or set of principles and deducing a conclusion logically from those principles. Creeds and dogmas are often deduced in this way by theologians. For example, John Calvin deduced from the premises that God is all-knowing and all-powerful the conclusion that He knows and controls every event in the world. Therefore, our fates are predetermined. If, as we tend to assume, religious people are (or at least should be) deductive thinkers, then every idea they hold, or every question they answer, should be restricted to logically deduced conclusions. Are they?

There are enough members of Calvin's Reformed Church tradition in Protestant Christianity today to constitute an excellent pool of experimental subjects. Not surprisingly, data regarding what they believe reveals that they don't believe this dogma very much at all (more accurately, they seem to believe it at some times but not others) even though, when asked, they will say that they do. Barrett has termed this phenomenon "theological correctness" because he found that Christians answer with systematic (i.e., "appropriate") answers when asked questions that allowed them to reflect at length on their beliefs, but they infer otherwise when asked different kinds of questions (in task-specific experiments) (J. L. Barrett 1999). So even Calvinists have beliefs that differ from Calvinist dogma dictates. Why? As I will show, it is quite natural to do so.

Theological incorrectness comes naturally to our brains because we spend much of our time thinking abductively. Abductive reasoning involves constructing general principles as explanations for particular events, such that if the principles are true, the event or phenomenon in question is explained. For example, imagine that person A, a Calvinist, is late for work and so speeds down the highway at a rate much faster than the legal limit allows. Person A is then suddenly forced to slow down because person B in front of her is driving very cautiously. Just as they approach an oncoming intersection, for which they have a green light, a drunk driver speeds through the red light from the adjacent street and kills person B. Saddened by the event, person A might say that person B's untimely death was a tragic piece of bad luck—but that by contrast, though, God (or one of God's servants, a minor superhuman agent like an angel, perhaps) was "watching out" for person A. In this hypothetical example, person A has reasoned abductively to conclusions that seem to contradict her otherwise held religious belief that God's divine sovereignty predetermines all fates.

This kind of thinking seems irrational to an outsider, but it comes quite naturally to the religious believer. We spend the majority of our time thinking abductively because abductive reasoning is efficient—it does the most work with the least effort in the shortest time. It explains everything that needs to be explained at the moment without forcing the person to go through all of the logical steps of deduction to produce an answer. As a result of its efficiency it is very useful for most of the everyday situations we encounter. In fact, this (likely) adaptive human capacity gives us an evolutionary advantage for survival. So it should come as no surprise that when we are forced to think religiously we employ the same means of economical explanation.

The study of human behavior that is rooted in the cognitive sciences, themselves rooted in evolutionary psychology, takes us a long way toward a sound and thorough understanding of religious behavior. Since religion, theological incorrectness included, is natural, we can employ a "naturalistic" approach to this study. In other words, theological incorrectness is susceptible to analysis by means of the methods employed by the natural sciences. Before I dig in, though, I should first traverse the treacherous terrain of widely held theories about religion so that I can identify and avoid many of their shortcomings. Students are often told that we study history to avoid its mistakes. The same principle applies here. In fact, that principle might be even more pertinent in the case of religion—for the events of September 11, 2001, reveal that our very lives might depend on us getting it right.

The Early Scientific Study of Religion

Historical perspective cautions us to proceed with humility. A scientific study of religion has been attempted before, but with considerable problems. Furthermore, using science to study religion is not uncontroversial (just like the scientific study of sexuality, virtue, violence, literature, art, or any other aspect of human life). Science and religion are thought to be separate domains; conventional wisdom even holds that they are antagonistic to one another. Science is descriptive—it limits itself to what we (can) know about the world. Religion, on the other hand, is prescriptive—it tells us what we should believe about the world. Religion deals with the "ought" (e.g., what we ought to think, what we ought to do, and so on). Science deals with the "is" (e.g., what a human's reproductive organ is, what racism is, what the process of photosynthesis entails, etc.). Often the two are incompatible, for you can neither deduce an "ought" from an "is" nor an "is" from an "ought" (Ridley 1997).

Of course there are some scientists who are religious and some religious people who embrace science, but these people seem to be in the minority. Many scientists (not to mention philosophers and, ironically, theologians) dismiss religion as nothing but superstition that results from not thinking about things properly. On the other hand, religious people often dismiss science as "meaningless"—a cold, heartless, and ultimately futile attempt to explain why things really happen. Religious insiders seek explanations of the big questions like "Where did we come from?" and "What happens to us when we die?" Scientists, in contrast, seek explanations for the small questions like "How do cells divide?" and "What happens when two elements are forcibly combined in a finite space?" Some people even go so far as to say that science offers nothing of important value to humanity because it cannot, in the minds of its critics, provide an ultimate cause. It is stuck in the world of proximate causes.

In other ways, however, religion and science are quite alike. Both require basic cognitive mechanisms to process data into representations of what the world seems to be like. And we see in both domains a difference between folk representations and reflective theories. Scientists tell us that the Earth is round and that the sun doesn't revolve around it even though we feel a flat Earth beneath our feet and watch the sun move through the sky each day. Similarly, God is not a person in the normal sense of the term (God doesn't need food and water to eat; God has no parents; God won't die a physical death; though male, God has no penis; etc.). Yet God is often thought of as an old man living in the clouds (interestingly, white people think of him as being white but blacks represent him as black). In this sense theology is to religion as actual science is to folk science. Furthermore, some scholars believe that just as science itself is susceptible to scientific analysis, so is religious behavior. The scientific study of religion makes religious ideas and actions the object of inquiry for the purposes of understanding the causal origins and functions of religion in our world. Keeping in line with the larger goals of science, such scholars believe that religion can be explained using the scientific method.

This is not the first and surely not the last attempt to use the scientific method to study religion. In fact people have been studying religion scientifically for over a century. Scholars in the nineteenth century generated many theories about religion that they believed identified its origin (history and causes) and functions. These scholars generated broad theories of religion as a cross-culturally recurring feature of human behavior. Their primary data sources were travelers who gathered information about the world's religions from oral stories, written texts, archaeological materials, personal observation, and so forth. That data revealed religions as having many similarities and of course many differences (mostly in content). In response to the growth of the sciences in Europe and the expansion of the "white man's world" into the so-called New World, the comparative scientific study of religion was born. This tradition provides inspiration and justification for the continued use of "methodological atheism" to study religion (Berger 1969). In other words, the early scholars of comparative religion believed that religion could be studied from an "outsider's" perspective, thus ignoring the truth or falsity of its claims.

Of course, like all sciences, much of what those scholars thought has been replaced over the years. In fact, most of what we once thought about religion is now considered false. However, the failures of these early scholars were of product, not process. In other words, they turned out to be mostly wrong in their conclusions but quite right in their general approach. To borrow a distinction from the cognitive sciences: explaining religion is a problem, not a mystery. This is good news because mysteries are insoluble but problems are tractable.

It has taken decades of serious scholarship to generate confidence that religion is a rightful object of scientific inquiry, and a perusal of the debates that got us to where we are today is illuminating. The scientific study of religion has accomplished three goals: (1) it has vastly improved our substantive knowledge of the contents of the world's religions; (2) it has generated theories about religious behavior at large that have given us a rich sense of why people all over the world believe religious ideas, perform religious actions, and join religious communities; and (3) it has allowed us to reflect on the consequences of religion on other aspects of our lives. Gained slowly but surely, these accomplishments have given us a better sense of what religion is all about.

The history of the study of religion reveals that from the late eighteenth to the early twentieth century scholars were divided into two camps over what religion was and therefore how we could account for it. These early "modernists" (labeled as such by "postmodernists" who came to the fore of the field in the 1970s) were one or the other of the following:

> *Naturalists:* those who believed that religion had natural origins, such as resulting from biological drives or intellectual attempts to explain the unexplainable.
> *Nonnaturalists:* those who believed that religion had nonnatural origins.

The nonnaturalists can be further divided into two subgroups:

> *Socioculturalists:* those who believed that religion was generated at the level of "society" or "culture."
> *Transcendalists* (sometimes called "supernaturalists"): those who believed that religion was a product of the human interaction with a supernatural reality, which was labeled variously as the "holy," the "numinous," or the "sacred."

In the remainder of this chapter, I will review the different approaches of paradigmatic scholars in each camp. The theories and methods they employed are diverse and interesting but, most important, instructive—thus putting us in a better position to understand the problems with folk psychological and with insider accounts of religion.

Social Science and the Enlightenment Paradigm

Scholars have only begun to scratch the surface of the very complex world of religious behavior, and yet what we do know is quite astonishing. In order to fully understand how we know what we know, we must go back to before the creation of a formalized scientific study of religion to the roots of science itself.

Although the human sciences began to mature with Charles Darwin's (1859) publication of *The Origin of Species*, the conceptual foundations of science at large are much older. Scholars have argued that the conceptual foundations of the scientific method were laid by Greek philosophers who believed, at least as early as the sixth century B.C.E. (but probably even earlier), that human beings were capable of formally figuring out on their own what the world is like (Pine 1989). Many of us take this capability for granted today (a sign of the impact of science on our world and, according to some pragmatist philosophers, of its truth), but it was revolutionary in its time. In that era, the leaders of religious guilds provided most people with explicit concepts of the world, though certainly not free of charge. Priests held, often with imperial or aristocratic support, a monopoly on conceptual models of the universe by claiming to have a pipeline to the gods. Generally speaking, all answers had to come from them (technically from the gods through them, but the effect was the same nonetheless) (Boyer 2001).

However, people like Socrates, Plato, and Aristotle, among other philosophers of the time, began to argue that human beings should doubt all unverifiable truth-claims (those that are either illogical or that contradict evidence). That is to say, people ought not to accept on blind faith everything that religious priests told them. Instead, these philosophers argued, humans should use their own abilities, which they called "reason," to figure out the world for themselves. This daring assertion would eventually change the world dramatically, because allegiance to the principle of doubt forces people to prove the truth of their beliefs. Making truth-claims susceptible to rigorous examination was the forerunner to the scientific method (Solomon & Higgins 1996).

Fast-forward to the seventeenth century. Philosophy, which had by then become an actual discipline of intellectuals who contemplated truth, value, the nature of the world, and so forth, had been weakened by the growing disbelief in the human ability actually to know anything about the world with certainty (it is, admittedly, a difficult task). One very important philosopher, however, dedicated his time to settling the matter of whether or not human minds could really know anything at all. In a flash of brilliance, René Descartes realized "Cogito ergo sum" (I think, therefore I am) (Descartes 1931). Descartes seemed to have proved that it is at least possible to know one thing for certain . . . that "I" exist . . . because something or someone (the "I") has to be asking the question "Do I exist?" In other words, knowledge of the act of thinking itself presumes that a thinker exists, and with that Descartes seemed to prove that we can know at least one thing. And if we can know one thing, why not everything?

This little phrase, which has since become famous (but not necessarily very well understood) throughout the Western world, had far-reaching implications. It launched an epistemological revolution (and soon afterward, several sociopolitical revolutions, in France and in the English colonies) as more and more Europeans began to have great, arguably exuberant, confidence that humans have what it takes (1) to figure out what the world we live in is like, and (2) to perfect that world. The movement known as the Enlightenment was born.

It didn't take long for scholars to begin developing instruments that could aid them in their pursuit of knowledge of facts about the world. Advances were eventually made in understanding of the basic laws of physics, chemistry, and even biology. Of course, once a few sound discoveries were made in these areas, people began to develop technologies that exploited that knowledge for human use (for better or worse). Thus, the creation of the "modern" world has a historical narrative: philosophy begat science, and with science we've changed the world.

The scientific method matured in the twentieth century when scientists began to fine-tune their methods of investigation and analysis (Kourany 1998). Ideally, the scientific method demanded (1) the generation of hypotheses about the cause(s) of some data (e.g., the stars follow the same path year after year because . . . ; humans stop bleeding after some time because . . . ; the United States of America is stratified because . . . ; etc.); (2) the gathering of empirical evidence about the phenomenon (often with the aid of instruments like the telescope, the microscope, and, later in the social sciences, questionnaires, surveys, and psychological experiments); (3) the creation of tests for the original hypotheses (e.g., X is hypothesized to cause Y; remove X, and Y should cease to exist); and (4) the publication of the tests' results to be scrutinized by professional peers (who often replicated experiments with different data or by a different method). Of course, in practice, science is not that smooth a process (Kuhn 1970). Mistakes are made; numbers are altered; scientific discoveries are rejected from publication because of personal animosity or political philosophy (like race or gender politics); biased inferences generate false hypotheses that nevertheless become accepted theories; and so forth. Yet the general method was established to the point that as the twentieth century began, we were poised to make truly significant discoveries about our world.

In this milieu, some scholars became interested in trying to apply the methods of the natural sciences to explain features of the human world. They established disciplines that became known as the "social sciences" (German: *geisteswissenschaft*; "science of the spirit"). Social scientists applied the scientific method to human behavior in the hopes of understanding why we do the sorts of things we do, and more prescriptively in the hopes of changing inappropriate behavior (Rosenberg 1997). Toward this end, psychologists studied the "psyche," or the mental processes that produced individual behavior, in order to eradicate mental illness (e.g., Freud 1946, 1961a, 1961b, 1967) or to cultivate self-actualization (e.g., Jung 1938, 1953–76). Sociologists studied group behavior to remedy social ills (e.g., Durkheim 1938, 1951, 1995; Weber 1958, 1992, 1993). Economists studied systems of exchange in hopes of eradicating class inequities (e.g., Marx & Engels 1964). Anthropologists studied other cultures to encourage the evolution and "civilization" of "primitive" cultures (e.g., Frazer 1911–15; Tylor 1903). These scholars hoped to discover the rules (i.e., laws) of human behavior worldwide so as to engineer utopian societies (although they often disagreed vehemently over what kinds of societies ought to be created).

Importantly, the social sciences emerged at the time of the growth of colonialism (the extension of European empires by colonizing the lands of the New World that had been discovered by explorers and traders from the fifteenth to the nineteenth century). Europeans used military force, politics, economics, and even cultural imposition as weapons in their efforts to subdue indigenous peoples (Said 1979). Large-scale ventures into Asia, Africa, and the Americas presented new challenges for social scientists in Europe. The discovery of other people with other religions, languages, skin colors, and so forth put pressure on European scholars to reconcile this new reality with prior ethnocentric assumptions. Europeans were forced by these experiences in "contact zones" (Pratt 1992) to confront and explain the existence of other social worlds. The reality of the existence of many cultures still challenges social scientists to this day, and that challenge has had an enormous influence on the academic study of religion.

Two paradoxical problems emerged in the crosscultural study of human behavior: (1) how to make sense of other people's profound dissimilarities, and (2) how to make sense of other people's profound similarities. Observant Europeans were struck by questions such as "Why don't other people believe in our God?" "Why don't they live in the same kinds of dwellings as we?" "Why do they eat different kinds of food?" We can safely bet that the natives were asking quite similar questions about the "white men" as well.

Others were struck by the numerous similarities shared by all people in all cultures. After all, the new discoveries of the colonial period suggested that people everywhere spoke some kind of language, practiced some kind of religion, and had some kind of self-governance. How could the existence of disparate but similar cultural systems be explained?

The scientific study of religion emerged in this context and therefore inherited many of the debates from the social sciences about human behavior. The scientific study of religion was important to the larger project of "the science of man" for three reasons: (1) science seemed to falsify religions' claims, and having a world full of false-thinkers was, to say the least, troublesome; (2) despite religion's archaism, it seemed to be ubiquitously tenacious; and (3) because of its falsity but ubiquity, it was at its best an impediment to progress, and at its worst dangerous.

One of the first efforts in the early scientific study of religion was to explain the underlying unity of all world religions. Some proceeded to do this by identifying its origins (in terms of its historical starting point and/or the causes that produce it) and its functions. Although scholars of religion disagreed over whether the underlying unity of religion was positive or negative for humanity, nearly all assumed it existed nonetheless. While later scholars (see chapter 2) would question the notion that all religion is essentially the same everywhere, most of the early scientific scholars of religion simply assumed that it was. In part, this was because they were committed to the general ideal of objectivity (that an "objective" world exists independent of our "subjective" representation of it). Unlike theologians, who insist that religion is best grasped from within a religious system (i.e., by accepting a few necessary assumptions), the modernist scholars of religion insisted that one could study religion from the outside (as a nonmember of the religion one studied). In fact, some believed that an outsider's perspective elucidated religion more clearly than an insider's position because the view from the inside is biased by the commitments of a culturally specific faith. In other words, insider views are often colored by the believer's motivation of securing the authenticity of that particular religion. The scientific study of religion began with these basic frameworks and assumptions.

Naturalist Theories

The scientific study of religion emerged within the social scientific study of human behavior in general. As mentioned earlier, there is some difference in orientation between the naturalists and the socioculturalist nonnaturalists, though both should be viewed as social scientific in approach. I review hereafter some of the most famous (or infamous, depending on your view) social scientific theories of religion, those of the anthropologists Edward Tylor and James Frazer, the economic critic Karl Marx, the sociologists Emile Durkheim and Max Weber, and the psychoanalyst Sigmund Freud. Each of these scholars was involved in disciplines with much broader concerns than religion. Each felt that any study of human behavior demanded attention to religion because religion is a ubiquitous and powerful presence in human affairs. Each of the social scientific approaches to religion in turn established subdisciplines within the academic study of religion: the anthropology of religion, the Marxist critical theory of religion, the sociology of religion, and the psychology of religion.

Identifying the internal properties of any given datum is an important step in the classification process of science (e.g., a penguin is [1] a bird [2] that doesn't fly, [3] lives in a cold climate, [4] eats fish, etc.). Consequently the search for a universal human nature and a corresponding definition of religion ran throughout the early scientific study of religion. Though the social scientists generally agreed that religion served important functions in human life, each put forth a different theory about what exactly that function was. Thus, social scientists are considered to be "functionalists" because religion, for them, was defined by its function. In the following sections, I will review the naturalists Tylor, Frazer, and Freud.

The Anthropological Naturalists

Edward Tylor (1903) and James Frazer (1911–15) are generally credited with establishing the anthropology of religion around the turn of the twentieth century. Most anthropologists at that time were adherents of some version of evolution put forth by post-Darwinian evolutionists. From Darwin's theory of natural selection they theorized that cultures also evolved from primitive/simple to modern/complex. This assumption, which later was shown to be quite simplistic, if not racist, dominated the early anthropological studies of religion.

Tylor and Frazer both assumed that religion had evolved from simple to complex in form and substance. They theorized that it must have originated as "animism" or "magic" and then morphed progressively into polytheism, monotheism, and agnosticism. Agnosticism in turn, they theorized, would eventually be replaced by pure scientific atheism. Using data about primitive religions gathered from travel writings, folk tales, oral stories, and so forth, these scholars argued that religion was something like a "folk science." Primitive men and women appealed to religious agents as a way to explain why otherwise unexplainable things happened in their world. For example, people stop moving, breathing, and so on when they die. Why this happens was perplexing (to say the least) to prescientific thinkers. So, according to Tylor and Frazer, primitive humans must have theorized that some kind of spirit (i.e., soul) animates each body for the duration of one's life and then departs at death. This primitive attempt to explain death constituted an intellectual attempt to make sense of the world. The Tylor/Frazer theory of religion is therefore referred to as the "intellectualist" theory because it assumes that religious beliefs provide explanations for unexplainable events like death.

The Psychoanalytical Naturalist

Sigmund Freud, the founder of modern psychoanalysis, theorized that religion was widespread because it served psychotherapeutic purposes such as neurotic outlet and wish-fulfillment (Freud 1946, 1961a, 1961b, 1967). For Freud, religion was nothing but the by-product of deeply rooted psychological conflicts between individual desires (what we want to do) and social rules (what we are allowed to do). Using data gathered from clinical psychotherapy, Freud hypothesized that religion soothes psychological discomforts such as the dissonance one feels about human mortality, about our powerlessness over the forces of nature, about repressed sexual desires, and so forth. Religion, he claimed, fulfills psychological needs such as the desire for a permanent father figure to protect us from bad things, the desire to be relieved of guilt, and so forth. Freud noted that religion often involves the "projection" of a father figure up in the sky somewhere who loves us, protects us, and rewards us if we behave but punishes us if we misbehave. Believing that there is a "big guy in the sky" to take care of us makes us feel better about our otherwise difficult and meaningless lives, but, warned Freud, believing in such illusions is nothing but immature, childlike "wish-fulfillment" that impedes healthy psychological growth. Religion is the illusion that all of our deepest wishes will be fulfilled if we just believe in the gods and perform the proper rituals.

Nonnaturalistic Social Scientific Theories

The Ideological Nonnaturalist

Karl Marx (though he worked with Friedrich Engels, Marx has gotten most of the credit for this approach, so I shall refer to their approach as "Marxist") argued that religion fulfilled the function of maintaining the socioeconomic status quo for the wealthy and powerful people (the "bourgeoisie"), such as the owners of businesses, land, money, and other forms of capital, by "naturalizing" (i.e., explaining) economic differences through religious myths. Religion was, according to Marx, an important pillar of the cultural "superstructure" (the noneconomic aspects of society) because it helped to maintain the basic economic disparities inherent in capitalism itself. Religion is very popular, he theorized, because it makes oppressed people feel better about their harsh lives by promising them rewards in an afterlife. "Religious distress," Marx wrote famously, "is at the same time the expression of real distress and the protest against real distress. Religion is the sigh of the oppressed creature, the heart of a heartless world, just as it is the spirit of a spiritless situation. It is the opium of the people" (Marx

& Engels 1964, p. 42). In other words, the masses turn to religion because it makes them feel good, for example, to think that their evil bosses will spend eternity in hell while they spend eternity in heaven. And above all poor people are comforted by the thought that life has some purpose to it—that it's all a part of "God's plan."

In turn, according to Marx, the bourgeoisie benefit from religion because it makes the working class passive. Religious dictates like "Thou shalt not kill" prevent people from taking the law into their own hands (e.g., overthrowing their bosses and taking over the industrial plants for themselves). In this way, religion maintains the status quo. People are kept in line by fear . . . of eternal damnation for breaking "God's" (i.e., the bourgeoisie's) laws. Religion, in this sense, functions as an effective tool of oppression (Marx & Engels 1964).

The Socioculturalists

By gathering data via macrosocial observation and statistical analysis, Emile Durkheim, the father of modern sociology, explained religion in terms of its social function: group cohesion (Durkheim 1938, 1951, 1995). Durkheim studied religious primitives, like the Australian Aborigines and the American Indians, because he believed they offered scholars a clear example of the earliest and therefore most basic form of religion, which he called "totemism." According to Durkheim's theory, human beings from birth live in social groups that constantly face the threat of internal disintegration (à la Freud's internal conflict). To prevent disintegration, the groups invent something to "cohere" them. One way that humans achieve group cohesion is to establish a group identity marker, a "totem," which represents the clan itself (e.g., the "coyote" clan, or the "fox" clan, or, to use a more recent example, Russia is represented by the bear and the United States by the eagle). Then they elevate the totem to the level of a deity in icons and in rituals, and construct prohibitive rules, "taboos," against its desecration. The group worships the totem (hence "totemism"), which for all practical purposes means that the group worships itself. This enhances an individual's identification with the group and thereby creates group cohesion.

Durkheim further theorized that rituals perform the important function of social indoctrination. When individuals participate in social rituals, they are transformed into social beings. They are educated about, invigorated by, what Durkheim called a mysterious process of "effervescence," and eventually are fully inducted into the group through uniformly established rites of passage. Thus, for Durkheim, religion has nothing to do with supernatural gods and everything to do with cohering social groups.

A second prominent sociological theory came from Max Weber (Weber 1958, 1992, 1993). Weber theorized, among other things, that religious ideas function as "ideal types," and ideal types motivate human action in the world (toward the achievement of the ideal). For example, Jesus established an ethical ideal type in the Sermon on the Mount (Matthew 5:1–7:27). Today, ideally, Christians strive to live up to this ideal (note the popularity of the "What Would Jesus Do?" paraphernalia). By encouraging followers to strive for the ideal, religion motivates social action and therefore engenders historical changes. Weber's most famous example of this was outlined in *The Protestant Work Ethic and the Spirit of Capitalism* (Weber 1992), in which he argued that the Western world (including the United States) progressed economically much faster than other cultures because the people in those societies were motivated by Calvinistic Protestant ideology. More specifically, according to Weber, Calvin's notion of "predestination" and the "doctrine of the elect" (i.e., those persons predestined for salvation) inspired hard work (i.e., the Protestant work ethic) because material success was considered a sign of divine favor and thus a sign of being a member of the elect. In other words, people worked hard, saved money, and excelled in capitalism because they were motivated by the theological doctrine of predestination. In short, according to this view, what people do is caused by what they think, which is in turn determined by the religious ideas they're taught.

Explanation Is Reduction: The Transcendentalist Response

What's important about these early social science approaches is their assumption that religion has little if anything to do with the gods. Instead, religion is a human invention that serves human purposes. In this sense the social scientific study of religion has been important not for what it proved but rather for what it started. It not only got the ball rolling in the study of religion but also spawned an important reactionary movement sympathetic to the idea that religion involved the supernatural. These nonnaturalistic reactionaries, whom I will call "transcendentalists," believed that there was much more to religion than just false beliefs or wish-fulfillment. Driven by this assumption, the transcendentalists established a separate discipline devoted entirely to the objective but sympathetic and comparative study of world religions. The transcendentalist approach eventually came to be called the "history of religions" in America. This approach is also referred to as the "Chicago school" because the first wave of scholarship about religion from professionally trained scholars of religion (Tylor, Frazer, Freud, Marx, Durkheim, and Weber were trained in other disciplines) came from the University of Chicago.

The pillar of the transcendentalist approach was that the naturalist theories were "reductionist" because they stripped religion of all its inherent religiousness. The social scientists seemed to think that religion was for dummies. In contrast, scholars like Rudolf Otto (e.g., Otto 1958), Joachim Wach (e.g., Wach 1944, 1951, 1958), and Mircea Eliade (e.g., Eliade 1954b, 1959, 1963a, 1963b, 1969, 1974), argued that religion was not only "holy" but in fact *sui generis*, or "of its own category." They argued that religion could not be explained entirely in the terms of anthropology, psychology, or any other social scientific discipline because religion was "irreducible." Mircea Eliade expressed this sentiment eloquently:

> A religious phenomenon will only be recognized as such if it is grasped at its own level, that is to say, if it is studied as something religious. To try to grasp the essence of such a phenomenon by means of physiology, psychology, sociology, economics, linguistics, art or any other study is false; it misses the one unique and irreducible element in it—the element of the sacred. (Eliade 1963b, p. xiii)

Although they disagreed with the naturalists' antireligious biases, the transcendentalists maintained the same modernist methods—gather data empirically, objectively classify and compare it, generate theories for the phenomenon, and then publish claims for peer review. Like the social scientists before them, the transcendentalists also championed the study of non-Western religions, which Eliade called (more respectfully) "archaic," not because they were the most simple but rather the most "pure" (i.e., uncorrupted by modern Western secularism).

Moreover, instead of focusing on religion's functions, they focused on the phenomenon of the experience of religion as expressed in the world's numerous sacred texts. They gathered primary data from the world's collective scriptures because these works were thought to capture religion's true "phenomenological" character—the multitude of experiences of the sacred. Once enough textual data was gathered, they were able to compare the canonical doctrines of the world's religions for the purposes of identifying an underlying unity of religious experience of what Rudolf Otto called *das Heilige*, or "the holy" (Otto 1958). By practicing *epoche*, which was a methodological strategy of "bracketing off" one's personal beliefs for the sake of looking at something from another person's point of view, the historian of religion hoped to come to a certain level of understanding and appreciation of all of the world's religious traditions, and ultimately (ideally) to synthesize and draw out the "religion" behind all religions. This, they hoped, would lead to an appreciation of the world religious traditions and possibly even to an awakening of humankind's true nature, the *homo religiosus* ("religious man"). More ethically concerned students of world religions even argued that the comparative study of the history of religion could lead to tolerance and respect for diverse peoples and cultures all over the world.

If religious traditions were the expressions of some basic sacred experience, and these expressions were to be gathered, compared, and interpreted (a method called "hermeneutics"), then scholars had to be trained in the original languages of the different world religions so that they could recover and translate the sacred texts in which these universal experiences were preserved. Thus, the history of religions approach was "textualist," in so far as it saw theology as being the most significant source of data to be unearthed and interpreted. The hermeneutic approach drove the transcendentalist study of religion for several decades, and to this day most textbooks on world religions contain surveys of texts that are assumed to present religion from the insider's point of view (e.g., Earhart 1993; Fisher 1991; Smith 1995).

From the textualist perspective, religions appear in history when special people have religious experiences and then communicate those experiences to other people in the forms of myths. Eliade, the most prolific transcendentalist in the Chicago school, called such sacred experiences "hierophanies"—instances when the sacred manifests itself on earth. Of course due to the nature of these experiences, they are nearly indescribable, which is why religious texts employ "symbolic" language (hence the need for professionally trained hermeneuticists to make sense of them). The expressions of people's experiences are then communicated among groups of people and culminate in the kinds of religious systems we recognize now—Buddhism, Christianity, Shinto, Wicca, and so on. Over time, the expressions of these religious experiences become the centers of debate, discussion, reflection, and so on, and so religious systems have developed "high" theological traditions that supplement myths and systematize worldviews. According to the transcendentalists, when studied comparatively these sorts of texts provide us with a glimpse of the sacred and therefore an orientation toward religiosity.

To Reduce or Romanticize?

Over the years scholars in these various theoretical camps have resorted to calling each other names. The naturalists have dubbed the socioculturalists "mystery-mongers" and the transcendentalists "romanticists" (Rosenberg 1997; Neilsen 1997). In retort, socioculturalists and transcendalists accuse naturalists of "reductionism." Regardless of metatheoretical stance, however, all of the early scholars of religion employed methods of investigation and analysis based squarely on the principles of the Enlightenment. At that time, this paradigm was considered the best approach to the study of religion because it was believed to be "objective." Social scientists felt confident in the objective methods of science to explain religion or even to explain religion *away*. Transcendentalists, on the other hand, while agreeing that the faith commitments of a theological approach restricted one's ability to study other religions objectively, felt that the social scientific approach (whether naturalist or socioculturalist) reduced religion to something not sacred. They argued in turn for the creation of an entirely different but nevertheless modern discipline dedicated solely to the sympathetic treatment of world religions. All seemed to agree, however, that the comparison of religions was not just possible but also necessary for a full and accurate assessment of the phenomenon (whether viewed romantically or reductionistically). In this vein, "to know one is to know none" became the mantra for the comparative study of religion (Müller 1873, 1878).

The employment of theories and methods rooted in the Enlightenment paradigm has earned these early scholars scorn in recent years. All of their approaches began to be lumped together as "modernist" (not a good thing) sometime around the 1970s, when the "cultural turn" (away from texts and ancient cultures) in the study of religion accompanied the ascension of postmodernism in the social sciences. Historians of religion had begun to realize that the textual approach to religion produced a narrow, idealized, and therefore inaccurate image of the world's religions. Many scholars, especially those interested in the religious lives of people left out of sacred texts like women, minorities, "subalterns" (Spivak 1994), and so forth therefore sought new methods for accessing the experiences of all religious people. Most of them turned to cultural anthropology where fieldwork studies of nonelites had been the focus of study for some time. Anthropological studies of culture had, by then, followed in the tradition of Durkheim and Weber more than that of Tylor or Frazer, in the sense that they came to see "culture" as being a dimension of reality that was distinct from the individual agents who collectively composed it. Whether they were conscious of it or not, postmodernist socioculturalists extended the assumptions of the early sociologists to their logical ends.

As scholars of religion made the cultural turn, the field of anthropology happened to be in the midst of a revolution in theory and method, the consequences of which had an enormous impact on the comparative study of religion. Cultural anthropologists were greeted in the 1960s with "postmodernism," an intellectual movement that challenged the foundational assumptions of the Enlightenment paradigm itself (Ortner 1994). Like the sophists of early Greek philosophy, postmodernists questioned the assumption taken for granted by modernists that the world was systematic and knowable by means of human reason. In large measure, due to their leftist sympathies with subalterns and their inherited (partly from the transcendentalists) disdain for science altogether, comparative religionists became excited by the postmodernists' criticisms. Many began to abandon "explanation" altogether, opting instead for "interpretations" of culture alone. Most famously, Clifford

Geertz (1973) argued that culture could (and should) be "read" like a text, an approach that fit well with the established hermeneutic tradition. This paradigm shift, if one is willing to grant that the Chicago school approach constituted a paradigm (see Kuhn 1970 for more on the notion of "paradigm"), came at a critical time in the discipline's history. Comparative religion was growing rapidly because many of the post–World War II teaching colleges were becoming full-fledged universities and so were hiring the new scholars of comparative religion being trained at the University of Chicago—precisely where Geertz was beginning to have an impact. As the students of religion at Chicago (and elsewhere later) were making the cultural turn in the study of religion, they were also starting programs at other colleges and universities throughout America. They took with them a combination of the traditional disdain for "scientific reductionism" (shared by the transcendentalists) as well as their newly formed disdain for "textualist" studies of religion that were said to "totalize," "essentialize," "idealize," and "obscure" "local" forms of religion that existed "on the ground." Their socioculturalist approach to religion has dominated the field for the past four decades and therefore constitutes the second wave of the "academic" study of religion (no longer able to be called "scientific" because of the conscious separation from explanatory endeavors).

The next chapter reviews the postmodernist nonnaturalist, and socioculturalist theories and methods of the study of religion and assesses their strengths and weaknesses. The work of second wave scholars has shed important new light on religion as it is actually practiced in the daily lives of living people (in addition to how religion is represented by sacred texts) and therefore given us new grist for our theoretical mills. However, this approach has been as much of a curse as a blessing. The assumptions about human behavior that accompany nonnaturalism (namely, that whatever we think and do is caused by culture) have limited its ability to explain the very behavior that its adherents have discovered.

CHAPTER TWO

RELIGION IS WHAT YOUR
PARENTS SAY

My wife is an elementary school teacher. Like most educators, she promotes the values of multiculturalism by beginning her social studies units with an "us-them-them" distinction. She might say something like "While we believe V, people F believe X, and people H believe Z." Her students have very little difficulty grasping this notion. Even for children, differences are self-evident.

Contemporary scholars of religion also tend to value multiculturalism. For them, it seems to go without saying that religion is "cultural." After all, where else could we get religion but by learning it from our parents, friends, and others in our society? There are many different religions, the logic goes, because there are many different cultures. Consider the titles of typical undergraduate religion courses: Religions of America; Religions of India; Japanese Religions; The Islamic Tradition; New Religious Movements; and so on. The multicultural approach to religion assumes that religious belief is determined by the culture in which it is located. Simple enough, right? Let's see.

Testing my wife's patience is always one confused or unruly child who defies this conventional wisdom by saying something like "People H actually like to use chopsticks? I have tried those things at the Chinese buffet where my dad takes us. But they are so hard to use, especially for rice and noodles. Forks are much better. I don't understand why people H still use those dumb things. Why are they so different from us?" The multicultural response, which can be characterized as "relativism," is, of course, "well, chopsticks are hard for you because you didn't grow up using them. People H have. So they prefer chopsticks to forks, which by the way they probably think are hard to use, too. What you have to remember is that people H are just different from us— not better or worse, just different. They use chopsticks and we use forks. It just depends on what you learn growing up."

This answer is "heuristically efficacious." In other words, it works, at least well enough to allow my wife to continue her lesson plans (and I suspect that it sounded correct to you). Once, however, while I was in a rather sassy mood, I challenged my wife on the answer. After some debate, she admitted, begrudgingly, that the response doesn't really answer the question. It actually dodges it. Of course, question-dodging is, understandably, sometimes necessary . . . as every parent and every teacher knows. Young children are insatiably curious, possibly even in infancy, as the developmental psychologists Alison Gopnik, Andrew Meltzoff, and Patricia Kuhl point out in their book *The Scientist in the Crib* (1999).

The answer "Because that's just what they do in their culture" sounds right because it fits well with the way we intuitively view the world. When we look around, proof for the theoretical notion that cultural properties are autonomous seems to be in the pudding. The sorts of values, preferences, attitudes, beliefs, and so on (e.g., preference for forks over chopsticks) that human beings possess seem to have been "picked up" from culture.

This common-sense notion has sophisticated scholarly kin—an approach to the study of human behavior that John Tooby and Leda Cosmides (1992) have called the "standard social science model." As we have seen, the idea that societies shape individuals is an old one dating back to Marx, Durkheim, and Weber. This assumption about human behavior is so powerful that the idea is simply accepted (arguably uncritically) as true beyond a reasonable doubt. Cultures cause behavior . . . and that's that.

However, one ought not settle for "that's that" answers. Let's approach this self-evident "truth" critically. If it is true, it will withstand the scrutiny. If it is not, we'll have to scrap it and begin anew.

The Standard Social Science Model

How do cultures cause individual behaviors, exactly? Most Americans learn in elementary school that a noun has to be a thing—you have to be able to touch it, feel it, smell, taste it, and so on. In other words, "things" have physical properties. Yet "culture" seems to be nonphysical. So how can "culture" exist if we cannot touch it, feel it, smell it, or taste it? Socioculturalists, like Clifford Geertz, say that culture has an abstract, "symbolic" existence. Geertz writes: "Believing, with Max Weber, that man is an animal suspended in webs of significance he himself has spun, I take culture to be those webs" (Geertz 1973, p. 5). Of course Geertz is speaking of "webs" metaphorically. Or is he?

Socioculturalists tend to be "dualists," insofar as they assume that certain "things" (like culture) exist outside of (or beyond) the physical world. "Stuff without material existence" makes, admittedly, for a fuzzy theory. And socioculturalists know this. The following admission by the socioculturalist Bruce Lincoln in *Guide to the Study of Religion* is telling:

> Let me begin by observing that although the term "culture" is a seemingly indispensable part of my professional and everyday vocabulary, whenever I have tried to think through just what it means or how and why we all use it, the exercise has proved both bewildering and frustrating. As a result, I am always on the lookout for serviceable alternatives and my list now includes such items as discourse, practice, ethos, *habitus*, ideology, hegemony, master narrative, canon, tradition, knowledge/power system, pattern of consumption and distinction, society, community, ethnicity, nation and race, all of which manage to specify some part of what is encompassed within the broader, but infinitely fuzzier category of "culture." (2000, p. 409)

As Lincoln's candor and his list of alternative terms suggests, "culture" is a term that's as clear as mud. Though we might use the term uncritically in our everyday conversations, it has quite a checkered history as a scholarly term (for more on the term's multivalence see Bourdieu 1993; de Certeau 1997a; Dirks, Eley, & Ortner 1994; Geertz 1973; Lincoln 1989, 2000; Nelson & Grossberg 1988; Sahlins 1976).

Understanding how culture is conceptualized and employed requires some unpacking. Maybe an example will help. As a child, my family belonged to a small evangelical Protestant church in the "Church of God" denomination that originated in Cleveland, Tennessee. In that church, women were discouraged from wearing slacks of any kind, wearing cosmetics, cutting their hair, sitting in the front pews (where men sat), and taking leadership roles in the church (other than bringing meals for unemployed church members, which unfortunately was common in that church). These discouragements constituted a set of rules that provided the church members with meaningful "webs of significance." The rules not only governed gender roles but shaped many of the members' attitudes, values, beliefs, and so on about human relationships, God's will, social mores, and so forth. These rules were not just known, they were "felt." I still recall the emotional discomfort people felt in the church when a female guest with short hair would come to a service wearing slacks and makeup and proceed to sit unknowingly in a pew in the men's section. Our church certainly had a "culture" of some sort.

One way of recognizing one's own culture is to leave it and to enter into a different culture (an experience many religion professors try to engender in the classroom). I became aware of our church's culture when in high school. I attended a service at my girlfriend's church, which was United Methodist—according to scholars of American religion, a "mainline" Protestant denomination (Roof & McKinney 1987; Williams 2001). Women in her church broke all the rules of my church. They cut their hair, they wore makeup and slacks, and they were not separated by gender.

The cultures of our respective churches were "symbolic" in the sense that the known but unwritten rules of conduct, behavior preferences, gender attitudes, values of segregation, and so forth had a powerful influence on the way people thought, felt, and acted. To use philosophical language, these church cultures "conditioned intentions." Unlike most nouns, then, culture is not defined by its essence but rather by its function. Culture is an important piece of the puzzle of understanding religion because of what it does to (or for) people.

As a supplement to the preceding example, here is Tooby and Cosmides's (1992) outline of the tenets of the standard social science model (SSSM). It is so insightful that it is worth listing in its entirety—all ten steps:

1. Culturalists assume a minimalist "psychic unity of mankind." In other words, "infants everywhere are born the same and have the same developmental potential, evolved psychology, or biological endowment" (p. 25).

2. "Although infants everywhere are the same, adults everywhere differ profoundly in their behavioral and mental organization." Culturalists deduce from this that "human nature (the evolved structure of the human mind) cannot be the cause of the mental organization of adult humans, their social systems, their culture, historical change, and so on" (pp. 25–26.)

3. "[Because] these complexly organized adult behaviors are absent from infants . . . they must 'acquire' it (i.e., mental organization) from some source outside themselves in the course of development" (p. 26).

4. "This mental organization is manifestly present in the social world in the form of the behavior and the public representations of other members of the local group . . . [a fact which] establish[es] that the social world is the cause of the mental organization of adults" (p. 26).

5. "The cultural and social elements that mold the individual precede the individual and are external to the individual. The mind did not create them; they created the mind" (p. 26).

6. "Accordingly, what complexly organizes and richly shapes the substance of human life—what is interesting and distinctive and, therefore, worth studying—is the variable pool of stuff that is usually referred to as 'culture' . . . variously described as behavior, traditions, knowledge, significant symbols, social facts, control programs, semiotic systems, information, social organization, social relations, economic relations, intentional worlds, or socially constructed realities" (p. 27).

Yet "if culture creates the individual, what creates culture?" (p. 27). The standard social science model answer is comprised of the final four tenets:

7. "The advocates of the Standard Social Science Model are united on what the artificer is not and where it is not: It is not in 'the individual'—in human nature or

evolved psychology—which, they assume, consists of nothing more than what the infant comes equipped with" (p. 27).

8. "The SSSM maintains that the generator of complex and meaningful organization in human life is some set of emergent processes whose determinants are realized at the group level. . . . The sociocultural level is a distinct, autonomous, and self-caused realm" (p. 28).

9. "Correspondingly, the SSSM denies that 'human nature'— the evolved architecture of the human mind—can play any notable role as a generator of significant organization in human life. In so doing, it . . . relegates the architecture of the human mind to the delimited role of embodying the 'capacity for culture.' [The human mind] is . . . [like] a general-purpose computer. Such a computer doesn't come preequipped with its own programs, but instead—and this is the essential point—it obtains the programs that tell it what to do from the outside, from 'culture' " (p. 29).

10. Finally, "in SSSM, the role of psychology is clear. Psychology is the discipline that studies the process of socialization and the set of mechanisms that comprise what anthropologists call 'the capacity for culture.' The central concept . . . is learning" (p. 29).

The insight for the student of religion is that if you want to know what religion is all about—if you want to know why people believe what they believe and do what they do—break it down by culture. Find out where people learned their religion. My high-school girlfriend's religion was significantly different from mine, despite the fact that we were both young white Protestant Christians from the same small town in the rural midwestern United States. Protestant Christianity is different in Biloxi, Mississippi, than in Boston, Massachusetts. Buddhism in Nepal is different from Buddhism in Boulder, Colorado. To say nothing of religion in Bangkok, Thailand, versus Zagreb, Croatia.

For socioculturalists, religion is a symbolic system of ideas governed by cultural rules specific to a particular group. Religion has a dual function: it provides people with a mental model of what the world is like—that is, a worldview—and an ethos that motivates behavior. It is a model of and for reality (Geertz 1973).

Thus, for Geertz and other socioculturalists, the study of religion should be interpretative because regional variance requires that we "get inside" the culture in question for the purpose of deciphering its symbolic rules. The best way to do this is through cultural immersion, because participant-observation allows us to construct a "thick description" (albeit synthetic) of what that culture is like by "translating" that culture's ways into terms familiar to us.

The standard social science model has its roots in the sociological frameworks of Marx, Durkheim, and Weber (Pals 1995). But, as I have shown, it was at one time merely one among three (along with naturalism and transcendentalism). It is now, however—at least in terms of the sheer number of scholars employing it—the dominant approach in the field. Why did this triumph occur? It is no coincidence that its ascendancy occurred in the 1960s.

To use the standard social science model to analyze the popularity of the standard social science model . . . just think of what American culture was like in the 1960s. Record numbers of American baby boomers flocked to colleges and universities as a means of upward social mobility or to avoid military service in the Vietnam war. Concurrently, college campuses throughout the country became hotbeds of the counterculture. Students—and professors alike—began to challenge many of the established ideas, values, and policies of "mainstream" American culture. The sixties were synonymous with the hippies and an ad hoc mixture of free love, rock-and-roll, mind-altering drugs, and of course, sociopolitical liberalism. It was (at least we romanticize that it was) revolution by day, bacchanalia by night.

For many scholars, the sixties also marked the end of confidence in both naturalistic and transcendentalists' textual approaches. Improved transportation made world travel more reliable and affordable, and exposure to other cultures began to reveal that textual studies of religion failed to capture religion as it is lived "on the ground." In many cases it was found that such scholarship even obscured or misrepresented people's actual religious beliefs and practices. In particular, the lives of subalterns (i.e. nonelites like women, minorities, etc.) were largely absent from the texts. Thus, scholars became sensitive to the experiences of subalterns and so turned to the study of the "living religions" of all people (e.g., Fisher 1991).

On the other hand, the socioculturalists maintained the transcendentalists' disdain for a naturalistic approach to religion on the grounds that science and religion were incompatible. Religion was "warm." It had to do with experience, meaning, worldview, and ethos. Science was "cold." It was about matter, objectivity, technology, and skepticism. Many humanistic scholars even began to fault science for the world's problems. The problems of war, racism, poverty, environmental destruction, and just about every other social ill could be laid at the doorsteps of science because of its apparent alliance with the mainstream. Science was too much a part of "the system."

In this milieu, many scholars of religion threw caution to the wind and made the "cultural turn" away from the frameworks of study established by their predecessors. They turned from texts (and minds) to cultures, especially cultures that were not mainstream ("the farther away the better"), for the purposes of painting a fuller picture of world religion. Also, the Hart-Celler Law allowed thousands of immigrants into the United States, exposing Americans to a host of spiritual alternatives to the established mainline denominational traditions (Roof & McKinney 1987; Wuthnow 1998).

Scholars of religion made this turn by embracing the theories and methods of cultural anthropology, which was undergoing a revolution of its own. Geertzian nonnaturalistic "cultural hermeneutics" was replacing one of the last remaining naturalist paradigms in anthropology, the structuralism of Claude Lévi-Strauss (Lévi-Strauss 1962, 1966, 1969). One of the central pillars of socioculturalism is respect for cultural autonomy (it is tempting to make the connection between this academic development and the "me" generation's sympathies for any group marginalized by the mainstream), and respect for cultural autonomy was supported by new philosophical claims being made by "postmodernists." Postmodernist socioculturalists criticized the naturalistic approach to anything social on the grounds that human behavior is motivated by intentions. Since intentions are viewed as "mental" (not material) phenomena, they cannot be susceptible to the methods of the natural sciences and their laws of natural causes (Rosenberg 1997).

I will now explore the postmodernist version of the standard social science model. In order to capture its spirit, I will employ its own language and style of argument. One can best understand its complexity by engaging its "discourse" (a term favored by postmodernists).

Postmodernism and Its Discontents

Postmodernism is an intellectual movement that heavily criticizes what it pejoratively dubs "modernism." Postmodernists sought (and still seek) to challenge the Enlightenment paradigm, including deconstructing the idea of objectivity and therefore all of science by extension. As one postmodernist quipped, postmodernism involves "an incredulity toward grand narratives" (Lyotard 1984). What modernists believed to be discovered truths were deconstructed by postmodernists as nothing but subjective, constructed, grand metanarrative discourses (plural) that were better analyzed as sociologies of knowledge. In postmodernism, all knowledge is assumed to be local, and so modernist theories are criticized for being "hegemonic." In fact, postmodernists hurl the label "scientism" at the efforts of scientists who parsimoniously explain the complexity of life in terms of causal laws.

Postmodernists seek to construct a pluralized image of the world that captures all of the ambiguities of the competing narratives of life. According to postmodernist conventional wisdom, human life is too complex to be studied scientifically ("humans are not atoms"), and thus they believe the concept of the underlying unity of anything human is highly suspect. They therefore advocate that the lines between social scientific disciplines that were created by modernistic university departments ought to be merged into, if not replaced altogether, by nonreductionistic humanities divisions. Scientific theories do not reflect reality per se, postmodernists argue. Rather, scientific theories are ideological constructions of religion that "signify" (a stay of political power) their view of the world. Science, in this view, is essentially no different from any other discourse that perpetuates power, and so the scientific search for causes (explanations) should be replaced by the critical evaluation of discourses (interpretations).

Eventually, the general postmodernist criticisms of modernism led to more specific socially concerned critical discourses about the consequences of modernism. Modernist theories were blamed for the political and economic power struggles of European colonialism and industrialization. Modernistic comparisons of people and cultures by privileged European male elites had led, they argued, to the "signification" of non-Europeans (Long 1986). At their best, discourses result in inaccurate images of other people that serve the purpose of constructing a self-identity vis-à-vis an imagined "Other." However, modernist discourses were often used to maintain the status quo or to subdue subalterns as part of Western patriarchal, ethnocentric, imperialist projects (Said 1979).

Postmodernist scholars of religion have in turn applied these criticisms of modernism to the study of religion. According to postmodernist scholars of religion, the methods and assumptions of the modernist study of religion constitute a rightful object of study themselves, because we need to "problematize" and deconstruct all modernist assertions. For example, the category of religion itself has been called into question as nothing but an abstraction that reflects not reality but merely the biases and assumptions of Western scholars operating in the modernist paradigm (Asad 1993; McCutcheon 1997; J. Z. Smith 1978, 1982, 1987, 1990). Other categories, like "ritual," for example, have been called into question and replaced with other terms, like "ritualization," which is believed to be more fruitful (Bell 1992).

Since all knowledge is "local," postmodernists like to localize and pluralize (Religion becomes religions; Culture becomes cultures, etc.), a move that has important methodological consequences. Weary of all grand narrative theories that oversimplify the complexities of life as lived on the ground, postmodernists encourage the acquisition of data by highly specialized studies of particular historical events. Assuming that all cultures are unique and autonomous, local area studies, in which students are encouraged to "go native," are favored over comparative studies (e.g., Ortner 1978). The goal of this kind of scholarship is arguably quite noble—to recover the voices of those left out of or misrepresented in texts and other repositories of modernist data for the purposes of creating a more "accurate and usable history" (Gross 1996). The greatest object of postmodernist scorn today is the armchair anthropologist or the canonical textolatrist. To combat such scholarly faux pas, graduate training now typically involves preparation for highly specialized studies of a particular group, a text (often noncanonical or popular), or a culture. Comparison is seen as abstract, superficial, and possibly dangerous.

Postmodernist scholars of religion also tend to blur the lines of analysis. Explanations of any kind have been replaced with subjective interpretations of cultural meanings, which themselves are viewed as multidimensional and shifting. Where "detachment" once reigned, subjectivity is now openly admitted, and so it is not uncommon to see books with introductory confessional chapters about the author's perspectives and biases (e.g., Gross 1993).

Overall, the postmodernist study of religion has sought in its more moderate forms to correct, and in its more extreme forms to deconstruct, the modernist study of religion by calling into question the Enlightenment paradigm itself, especially its foundational principle of objectivity. Since knowledge is constructed, postmodernists believe, all knowledge must be seen as local, particularized, perspectival, political, and so forth. Furthermore, being mindful of the legacy of modernism, postmodernists argue that we must be diligently reflexive about what we say. In fact, we might do more good undoing the wrongdoings of modernism than trying to make any constructive claims at all. Simply put, because we are incapable of being truly objective, subjectivity renders all comparison superficial and unacceptable. All events, including religious ones, are unique, so postmodernists eschew comparisons.

The Method in the Madness

I have tried my best to stay true to the spirit of postmodernism in the preceding section. I apologize if I confused you, but postmodernist jargon is often unclear. To be fair, however, postmodernists will retort that vagueness is more representative of the messiness of life than simplistic scientific theories, which mask complexity. Postmodernism's infamous unintelligibility inspired Ernest Gellner to dub it "metatwaddle" (Gellner 1992, p. 41). But there is method to its madness. In fact, it turns out to be quite intelligible, even quite simple. Perhaps a translation into "common" English will help.

Postmodernism began in Europe primarily among literary critics and philosophers with complicated roots in various disciplines such as poststructuralism, phenomenology, and critical theory. It emerged in America when the cultural turn was made by Geertz. Geertz popularized interpretive symbolic anthropology as the most promising method for the study of religion because of its "holism" (Pals 1995). According to Geertz, to understand why people do what they do, one has to identify the intentions behind their actions and then decipher the internal coherency of the cultural rules that condition intentions (Geertz 1973; Rosenberg 1997). For example, right now I am typing on my keyboard with the intention of creating a coherent story about the logic of postmodernism. Were someone to study me, they might look beyond that surface level intention I just offered and infer instead that what I really am doing is inventing a story from my personal experiences for the purposes of advancing my academic career. To accomplish this, they might argue, I am constructing a discourse that sets me apart from other people and thus increases my value as a writer. (The more I confuse you, the smarter I appear!) Why do I do this? Because I am a self-interested white heterosexual privileged Protestant male who uses knowledge for power (a strategy not of savvy but of manipulation and exploitation). For postmodernists, that which gets presented as truth (e.g., this book) is an invention, just a take on reality, that masks what I am really doing—tricking everyone in order to acquire and maintain power.

You might have noticed, by now, that postmodernism is a sophisticated form of cultural Marxism. Keeping in line with Marxist analysis, postmodernists propose two levels of scholarship: thick description and discourse criticism. In other words, the study of culture should involve (1) finding out how a culture works by identifying its webs of significance (e.g., college professors in the United States are chosen among a pool of graduate students who must play by the rules of the game and write a book that claims to know something very important that no one else knows), and then (2) criticizing its power structures for their oppression of subalterns (e.g., this is why minorities are underrepresented in academia—it is because the discourse is controlled by the intellectual bourgeoisie) (e.g., Lincoln 1989). One should be able to see how religion is implicated in this system—not only is religion a discourse of power, so is the study of it (e.g., Asad 1993)!

Does postmodernism unveil the true motives of scholars who, like Enron executives, don't want others to know? Does it explain culture? The answer is . . . no. Of course, I have little doubt that scholars have personal interests. What I doubt, however, is that culture causes them to be this way (or that way, assuming the postmodernists, as critics of "the system," imagine their liberal ideology to be superior [but are they masking masking?!]). Philosophically speaking, postmodernists have not explained anything. They have merely restated the question and affirmed the consequences. Thinking back to my wife's unruly student: why do some people like rice and others like pizza? To say it's because their culture is different begs the question of why their culture is different.

There are serious flaws with the postmodernist sociocultural approach to religion. So I will be critical of the critics. I will de-construct deconstructionism.

Deconstructing Postmodernism and the Standard Social Science Model

A recent approach to the study of religion, which I will call "neo-modernism," has revived but modified the basic principles of early modernism and offered a retort to postmodernism. The modifications to modernism by neomodernists are few but significant. The criticisms of postmodernism are also significant but are not few. I will address each in turn and then sum up the criticism of both within the neomodernist model, which is an outgrowth of the "cognitive revolution" (Thagard 1995).

The primary criticism of early modernism by neomodernists is that while it was on the right track, it failed to adhere to its own standards. That is, unlike the postmodernist criticisms of modernism, neomodernists argue that the early modernists were simply not scientific enough. Either because of their personal political philosophies or because they were an accident in time (they simply didn't know what we know), the early modernists operated on fundamentally flawed assumptions about human behavior. Further-more, by maintaining that religion was *sui generis*, the transcenden-talists cut themselves off from science and implicitly forwarded a theological agenda (albeit a liberal one, which is implied as [more] acceptable).

Of the reductionists, Durkheim—the foundational representative of the standard social science model—has received the most criti-cism from neomodernists (Tooby & Cosmides 1992). Durkheimian sociology assumed that group behavior constituted "social facts" and therefore should be studied independently of biology or psy-chology (Durkheim 1938). Operating under the mind-blind illu-sion of cultural autonomy, he (and many others who followed) cut himself off from fruitful discussions with scientists operating at cognitive levels of analysis. To this day, socioculturalists tend to view culture as existing on some kind of astral plane independent of the human agents that produce and transmit it (Sperber 1996). This restricts the ability of the sociologist to provide grounded ex-planations for human behavior and to make powerful predictions about group behavior.

On the other hand, anthropology has always been troubled by

its early misuse of Darwinian anthropology. While the Frazor/Ty-lorian intellectualists assumed that religion had something to do with thinking, they were biased by "social Darwinism" and so concluded unscientifically that religions evolve from simple to complex. Furthermore, they were hampered by limited crosscultural data. Much of what they did have was obtained from travel writings that were sensationalized and therefore unreliable (Pratt 1992). This meant that they lacked a thorough selection from which to theorize comparatively. In large measure, postmodernists have sought to correct the early racisms of anthropology, but unfortunately they have gone too far in emphasizing that all ideas are to be respected as equally valid. This creates a paradox in postmodernism—all ideas, except modernist ones, are valid.

Freud was partially correct to assume that cultural behavior is the collective output of mental processes, which in turn are constrained by evolution. However, his tripartite theory of mind has proven to be wrong (or at least intractable). Like all of the early modernists, Freud inferred theories about the "hidden" functions of the mind that were not testable.

Furthermore, the antireligion bias of these early reductionists led them to abandon the principles of objectivity. Their reductionism was motivated by a desire to explain religion away rather than just to explain it at a cognitive level of analysis (i.e., from culture to cognition). By analogy, instead of merely studying how the eye works to understand how a person perceives a painting as beautiful, these early scholars wanted to get rid of the experience of beauty altogether (Damasio 1994). They wanted to make the painting go away. Unfortunately, as a result, reductionism is still a dirty word in many circles.

On the other hand, the transcendentalists were correct in wanting to compare religions for the purposes of identifying the underlying unity or structure of religious thought and behavior. However, by losing touch with discoveries in other important related fields (because they demanded to be a *sui generis* discipline), they severely limited their ability to do so. Eliade and his colleagues left students with only one option—either you see religion romantically (as an "orientation toward the sacred") or you don't. Such a position violates the principle of Occam's razor, which stipulates that we should posit the minimum amount of entities that are necessary for explaining a phenomenon (Solomon & Higgins 1996). It also commits one to a theological agenda. Scholars of religion, I believe, do not need to know whether or not God exists to study religion. Thus, while our descriptive knowledge of the world's religions has been expanded by the work of historians of religion, our fundamental knowledge of why religion is a recurrent feature of human behavior has not.

In addition to the criticisms of early modernism, there are at least six (by my count) neomodernist criticisms of postmodernism. First, while postmodernism should be appreciated for its corrective criticisms of the early modernist weaknesses, its claims of deconstructing objectivity and science are specious, if not fraudulent. Postmodernists have drawn a straw man in "scientism." The overwhelming successes of the natural sciences, especially the recent advances in biology, cannot be ignored or dismissed as coincidences or lucky guesses. As it turns out, science is a kind of knowledge that is fundamentally different from, for example, religious ideas (for one thing, scientific theories are falsifiable) (Mc-Cauley 2000a). Science has proven over and over again that it can construct powerful and predictive theories about the world and its workings, including human behavior. The primary reason why the humanities and social sciences have not enjoyed the same success is because they have cut themselves off from the wealth of knowledge that can be generated by the methods of the natural sciences. Postmodernists misunderstand what science does. It is not a panacea that seeks the certainty of explaining everything. Rather, the scientific method allows scholars to reduce complexity down one level at a time, thereby enabling scholars to unify claims. Importantly, doubt is the hallmark of science. Knowledge advances "one funeral at a time" (E. O. Wilson 1998).

Second, because of the biophobia in the humanities and other related social sciences, socioculturalist scholars of religion produce scholarship that turns out to be little more than journalism. Their job is "getting the story." Mere description is ultimately intellectually unsatisfying, however, and it offers little to academia and to students. The result has been the widespread institutionalization of the "zoo" approach in religion departments, in which each religious story is told in individual offices and content-specific classes (again, Religions of Japan, Religions of Africa, Religions of India, etc.). Explaining religion takes a back seat (or is put in the trunk) to learning about religions, as if learning a foreign language excludes theorizing about grammar. While this approach might be convenient and serve the particular curiosities of individual students and scholars, how much can one learn at the zoo?

Third, postmodernists wrongly assume a minimalist theory of

mind: that human minds are little more than culture sponges—or "black boxes," in B. F. Skinner's (1953) famous stimulus-response model of behaviorism—that are just sophisticated enough to pick up what the senses experience. For example, one is taught to understand Buddhism in "historical contexts" because, the theory assumes, human behavior is the product of environment and historical antecedents.

This assumption is logically flawed. If humans are products of culture, then how is culture ever generated or changed? The philosopher Immanuel Kant pointed out years ago that something (what he called "a priori categories") must undergird our perceptions, or else knowledge and communication of any kind would be impossible (Kant 1929). Cognitive scientists have argued persuasively that our minds are not content-free *tabula rasas* but rather are content-rich information processors that are predisposed to bias reality in certain ways (Chomsky 1957, 1972, 1986; Pinker 1997; Thagard 1995, 1998; Tooby & Cosmides 1992). Cultures have recurring features—such as religion, art, music, language, and so on—because humans actively generate and transmit ideas and actions. The focus on cultural analysis alone obscures the underlying unity of behavior that is susceptible to analysis at the level of cognition. Thus, we can compare religions by starting with the assumption that human beings across cultures are quite similar.

Fourth, postmodernism's claim that all knowledge is local is illogical. If all knowledge is local and thus subjective, then we can't take seriously the claim that all knowledge is local and thus subjective . . . because that claim itself is merely local and subjective. It's like the paradox from the philosophy of language . . . the sentence, "I am lying." If true, it's false. If false, it's true.

Fifth, because they have distanced themselves from science, postmodernists often work in the humanities and so enjoy a lack of constraining principles on their claims. Almost anything goes, as long as it is in vogue, because the validity of claims made can only be evaluated subjectively. The unfortunate by-product of this is that authority is manufactured by pedigree. Without any constraining theoretical or methodological principles, the field is subject to faddish trends in which the most popular ideology or political philosophy reigns. What is true, and this is another postmodernist paradox, is whatever is in fashion (e.g., postmodernism).

Finally, the reigning ethical philosophy in postmodernism has been cultural relativism (what I started off calling "multicultural-ism"). According to this position, no ideology is inherently any better than any other. As I said earlier, this might be an attractive plea for tolerance, but it is ultimately untenable. Again, if it is true, then it disproves itself. How is any scholar's claim evaluated? Moreover, how do we decide whether, for example, capitalism is better or worse than socialism? By what criteria would slavery be wrong? How do we determine whether Egyptian youth clitorec-tomies are wrong or just part of that culture? This untenable po-sition of cultural relativism has been exposed as fundamentally problematic in the wake of the tragic attacks on the World Trade Center on September 11, 2001. Some ideas and actions are worse than others.

To conclude, we should be balanced in our assessment of the standard social science model and of postmodernism. The recent socioculturalist emphasis on gathering ethnographic data has been a blessing, insofar as the data have greatly improved our substantive knowledge of world religions. We know a lot more about the ac-tual contents of religious systems, and how those contents vary from person to person, group to group, culture to culture, now than we once did. Yet new data is not new knowledge. The the-oretical inadequacies of the standard social science model have limited its explanatory power. We simply have not done a very good job of making sense of the data. We know what, but we haven't done much to explain why. So, rather than abandoning modernism altogether, we should have corrected its flaws. Instead, nearsighted scholars have accepted deeply problematic assumptions about knowledge, scholarship, cultures, religion, and human be-havior from postmodernism. That has prohibited progress in the field.

Fortunately, a new model has emerged that has been remarka-bly successful in explaining much of what the data reveals. The interdisciplinary field known as the cognitive sciences explains hu-man behavior in terms of the processes of thinking that generate behavior. Since thinking is a function of the brain, we can apply naturalistic models of explanation. For brain matter matters a great deal.

Chapter 3 reviews the final and, as I said earlier, the best method we have for studying religion. The establishment of the cognitive sciences truly represents a revolution in the study of hu-man behavior and as such deserves its own chapter.

CHAPTER THREE

RELIGION IS PERFECTLY NATURAL,
NOT NATURALLY PERFECT

Gods aren't very good conversation partners. They're aloof. They ignore you. They're unreliable (at least by human standards). Gods seem to have minds of their own.

Religions are "self-referential" systems. In other words, the objects to which the systems refer, that is, gods, aren't present in any normal sense of the term. This poses a unique problem for the study of religion that scholars of, say, economics, gender, or politics don't face. When human beings pray to a god, make offerings to a goddess, cast out demons, run from ghosts, and so forth, the object of the action is imagined. The objects of religious thought are, to use a technical term from the cognitive sciences, "representations."

This is not to say that the objects to which the representations refer do not exist (who knows?!). Imagine for a moment that your best friend is sitting at a local café and sipping a strong cup of coffee. You just imagined something that could be very real, but your imagination of it was nonetheless a representation. Now imagine that your friend is a dinosaur, say a Tyrannosaurus rex, hanging upside down from the limb of a rainbow-striped tree. You've just imagined something that does not exist, but you imagined it nonetheless. And both representations came to you naturally. You didn't have to strain a bit—your brain represented both quite easily. In this sense, your representations are "real" because they have tractable mental properties.

The content-claims of religious systems are peripheral to the actual object of study in the cognitive science of religion. We are more interested in the operations of the cognitive mechanisms that produce, constrain, and transmit religious representations than in whether those representations refer to external realities. Whether or not gods exist makes little or no difference at all to the study of the brain mechanisms that are involved in the production of religious thoughts and performance of religious actions. Cognition, which Tom Lawson has defined as "the set of processes by which we come to know the world," is the object of study. Thus cognitive science, again to use Lawson's language, "is the set of disciplines which investigate these processes and propose explanatory theories about them" (Lawson 2000, p. 75).

The cognitive approach to religion is a "naturalness" thesis because cognitive scientists believe that religion is a by-product of the processes of ordinary human cognition. In other words, cognition operates in such a manner that religious representations emerge quite naturally as an aspect of ordinary thinking. So religious thinking, like thinking about dinosaurs in rainbow-striped trees, is quite natural (J. L. Barrett 2000). The brain that balances your checkbook, enjoys looking at pictures, cheers for football teams, and much more is the same brain that enables us to pray to gods, make offerings to goddesses, cast out of demons, and be scared of ghosts. With that in mind I will now provide brief reviews of the central theories in the field, which will allow me to synthesize the material to explain why religious people believe what they shouldn't.

The Cognitive Revolution

It is hard to pinpoint the beginnings of the cognitive sciences. Owen Flanagan (1991) has argued that the cognitive sciences had many predecessors, like Aristotle, Descartes, Kant, William James, Freud, Jean Piaget, Lawrence Kohlberg, and so on, who contributed to its development. Among the many people we could credit with having founded cognitive science, one solid candidate is Noam Chomsky. Chomsky argued that human beings learn language from culture because of the way the brain works not because of the way culture works (Chomsky 1957, 1965, 1972, 1975, 1980, 1986, 1993). In this regard his work was foundational because later cognitive scientists were able, by drawing on his work, to confidently claim that culture works the way it does because of the brain, not the other way around (Boyer 1994, 2001; Lawson & McCauley 1990; McCauley & Lawson 2002; Sperber 1975, 1996). The prevailing assumption about language acquisition during Chomsky's early career was that it was "behavioral," meaning that children learn to speak and comprehend language by memorizing and imitating the thousands of sounds, words, sentences, and so forth heard in their environment. For example, Mommy points at the poodle and says, "Dog." Child points at the poodle and says, "Dod." Close enough. The child's mimicry reveals that she or he has gotten it. Simply continue to add more and more words to the little child's sponge-like "black box" and you've got the makings of an active language. This behavioral picture of how we learn languages seems, like other sociocultural theories of learning, to be self-evident. Why else do children raised in the United States say "Hello, friend!" while those in Bangkok say "Sawasdee khrap/khaa!" and those in Tokyo say "Konneechi-waa!"

Chomsky did not fully accept this "self-evident" process, though. He was uncomfortable with some of the puzzles that this model of language acquisition presented. For example, say the following sentence to yourself: "My invisible blue waterbug eats backward." You just learned a new sentence, which most likely has never been spoken before. By having you say this sentence, however, I've created a problem. The problem is that I made it up. Yes, that's right. I completely invented that sentence. I've never once heard that particular sentence in my life. So what's the problem with that? Well, if language is "picked up" from speakers around us, then how are novel sentences ever *generated*? How is it that I can produce a sentence that I've never heard?

Well, you might say, all you have to do is memorize new words and put them together in strings to get new sentences. That's a logical guess, but it doesn't explain *how* one knows how to put the words together in the first place. How do you know where the words go?

Chomsky noticed that language speakers in all cultures have a fairly comfortable grasp of syntax. Yet no one ever learns the rules of syntax. Thus, he hypothesized, since humans have the capacity to generate (not just imitate) language, "syntactic structures" must be constrained by cognition (Chomsky 1957). Chomsky demonstrated that words function as representations in our mind-brains.

A word is something like a "symbol," insofar as the word "water-bug" stands for the animal that speakers of the English language call a "waterbug." Thus words are representations of the kinds of things that are in the world. Furthermore, words can represent either things (nouns) or actions (verbs). Once a word is "cata-logued" by your brain as a thing or an action, the brain is then able to put it in its proper place in a sentence. Even though I had never heard the aforementioned sentence, I knew instinctively how to say it. And because our brains are genetically similar, it probably sounded (syntactically) normal to you.

Here's a second puzzle of the sociocultural acquisition of language thesis. Five minutes or so after the child, I'll call her Betsy, points at the poodle and says, "Dod," she points to the chair and says, "Dod." Then Betsy points to the cat and says, "Dod." And then Betsy points to Mommy and says, "Dod." To the dismay of her parents, Betsy seems to think that everything is a dog! What's the problem (for the purpose here)? The problem is that Betsy is thinking. Even though by adult standards she is not thinking ac-curately, nevertheless she is not simply regurgitating a referential term. She has internalized a word that has some reference in the world, but she seems intent to choose object(s) to refer to that are not in line with what the parent teaches her is a dog. If humans were merely language sponges (or culture sponges, for that matter), then why would little kids the world over make the mistake of confusing "dog" with "cat" or "road" or anything else?

Here is another puzzle. Eventually, Betsy will develop to the point in which parents will cease to "baby talk" with her. They will stop enunciating to emphasize ("Beeeetsy. Daddy looooves you. You love Daddy, dooooooon't you? Yeeeeeeees, you loooooooove Daddy.") They will also end their use of unintelli-gible gibberish ("Oooohh. Wittow woo-woo. Aaaah, gitcha gitcha gooo-gooo"). And they will stop completing their sentences; they won't say every word needed to finish the sentence. Here are some examples. See if you can finish these thoughts:

1. If you cheat you'll get . . .
2. No! Don't you even . . .
3. What is the name of that man on that TV show who . . .
4. Life is like a box of . . .

More than likely, you are able to come up with words to finish my thoughts. How can you do that? We are not even in the same room together, yet you can infer what I am intending to say. What a miracle!

If language acquisition is word by word, then fragments could not be completed by a listener, at least not as easily and accurately as we do in our everyday lives. Obviously, something is going on in the brain that is much more complicated than merely "picking up" language from culture. Language performance involves thinking, and thinking involves the processes of cognition.

Finally, consider this. Anyone who has studied Thai or Japanese knows that "Sawasdee khrap/khaa," and "Konneechi-waa" mean roughly the same thing as "Hello, friend." Anyone who has studied French would know that "Bonjour" means the same thing as well. In Spanish it's "Hola"; Italian, "Buongiorno"; Chinese, "Ni-hao"; Hindi, "Namaste"; and German, "Guten tag." How is it that these languages all share the same concepts? How is it possible to translate languages into another? If all languages are different, then translation should not be possible at all. Yet we do it all the time (some of us better than others . . . though effort plays a role in that).

All of these puzzling facts point to one conclusion: human brains are very active in the language process. We can utter and understand novel sentences. We can make referential mistakes with words. We can complete others' incomplete thoughts, and we can translate from one language into another.

These sorts of clues led Chomsky to reevaluate what linguists had long thought about the processes of language acquisition. Eventually, Chomsky postulated that the brain must come pre-wired for language with what he called a language acquisition device (LAD). There could be no other explanation, he reasoned, for the striking fact that there is complete (as far as anyone can tell) universality of these, and other, recurrent features of language. Chomsky's LAD theory, like many theories in a budding science, was later shown to have problems. In fact, an intellectual battle continues to be fought between "East Coast classicalists" (those who believe that much of our cognitive capacities are in place at birth or emerge very early on) and "West Coast connectionists" (those who believe that cognitive capacities develop over time) (Pinker 2002). Nevertheless, Chomsky ignited a cognitive revolution by showing that human behavior is not simply a product of culture. Human brains are much more active in the transmission of cultural products than the socioculturalists assumed. Of course cultural products play a very important role in learning and behavior, but cultural products are only one side of the behavioral coin.

Chomsky's theories were a watershed for our understanding of behavior because they showed that through focused reasoning and carefully designed experiments, scholars could "map the mind" (the "mind" is a shortcut term for our cognitive system[s]) (Hirschfeld & Gelman 1994). This also meant that naturalism was back in the human sciences because Chomsky made it clear that intentions, the pillar of the nonnaturalists' criticisms of naturalistic approaches to human behavior, had tractable properties.

I must admit that I have been oversimplifying Chomsky's very complex arguments and evidence for the cognitive basis of language (and all behavior). The point has been to show you the key feature of cognitive science: that the brain is chock full of structures that constrain the way humans behave. This means we can use science to study humans after all, because humans are physical things that function according to causal laws.

Cognition, Culture, and the Study of Religion

As I said earlier, few cognitive scientists still believe Chomsky's theory of LAD. Nonetheless, nearly all believe his general approach was the best method we've generated thus far for explaining human behavior. We have great confidence in this stance because many other theories, and much more evidence, followed Chomsky from a variety of fields. Cognitive science is necessarily interdisciplinary, because cognition is responsible for how we think (philosophy and psychology) in all cultures (anthropology) according to tractable information-processing rules (artificial intelligence) that cover all aspects of human life: art, music, literature, and so on, and of course religion.

The application of a cognitive approach to cultural-symbolic systems was established in large measure by Dan Sperber's book *Rethinking Symbolism* (1975). Sperber offered an insight about symbolic representations that would play an essential role in the cognitive science of religion: the proper object of the study of culture should be the mechanisms that produce and transmit symbols rather than the meanings (which are, because of their multivalence, interpretive nightmares) of the symbols themselves. For what is culture other than the collective outputs of human mental representations that spread and stick in a given population?

> Just as one can say that a human population is inhabited by a much larger population of viruses, so one can say that it is inhabited by a much larger population of mental representations. Most of these representations are found in only one individual. Some, however, get communicated: that is, first transformed by the communicator into public representations, and then retransformed by the audience into mental representations. A very small proportion of these communicated representations get communicated repeatedly. Through communication (or, in other cases, imitation), some representations spread out in a human population, and may end up being instantiated in every member of the population for several generations. Such widespread and enduring representations are paradigmatic cases of cultural representations. (Sperber 1996, p. 25)

What follows from this insight for students of religion is remarkable. It shows us that religious systems are susceptible to cognitive analysis because they are products of mind-brain processes. In this vein, the earliest attempts at a cognitive approach to religious behavior consisted of research in the subfield of social psychology known as attribution theory. In general, attribution theories assume that a fundamental human capacity is the "propensity to make sense of the world, to understand the causes of events" (Spilka & Schmidt 1983, p. 326). Naturally, attribution theories have implications for the psychology of religion because religious ideas provide believers with causal explanations of the world's workings. The earliest attempt at an attribution theory for the study of religion was offered by Wayne Proudfoot and Phillip Shaver (Proudfoot & Shaver 1975). However, research during the 1980s and 1990s generated a robust body of knowledge about how, when, and why humans make supernatural attributions (Lupfer, Brock, & DePaola 1992; Lupfer, DePaola, Brock, & Clement 1994; Lupfer, Tolliver, & Jackson 1996; Spilka & Schmidt 1983; Spilka, Shaver, & Kirkpatrick 1985).

Drawing on results from experiments in which participants were read event stories and asked to infer the likeliest causes of the events in the stories, researchers found that humans are more likely to employ supernatural attributions as causes of events for the following reasons: if one is personally affected by an event; if the event is significantly important; if the event has a positive (rather than negative) impact; and/or if the event is of a health-

or finance-related concern. Furthermore, the attribution theory research revealed that humans generate supernatural attributions when they provide meaningful explanations of events, when they allow the attributor to gain a sense of prediction and control of events, and/or when they improve the self-esteem of the attributor (Spilka & Schmidt 1983; Spilka et al. 1985). Hence a supernatural explanation is likely to be invoked if, for example, a person's terminal illness is suddenly cured (miraculously).

Later attribution studies nuanced the claims by Spilka and his colleagues. Lupfer and his colleagues showed that some humans make supernatural attributions for everyday behavior as well (Lupfer et al. 1992; Lupfer et al. 1994; Lupfer et al. 1996). Supernatural attributions are made for everyday behavior (e.g., saying a simple prayer of thanks at dinner) if the attributor possesses in memory supernatural concepts that are "readily available." Typically, devoutly religious people who spend a great deal of time and energy learning and employing religious concepts have readily available conceptual schemes at their cognitive disposal. In other words, devoutly religious people maintain religious (mental) models of the world, and therefore such people are able to access such concepts for causal explanations on a regular basis. However, even religious attributions for everyday behavior made by devoutly religious people are constrained by cognition. The experiments performed by Lupfer and his colleagues revealed that religious attributions for everyday behaviors were made more often when the attributor was a devout believer and the event to be explained was personally significant.

This literature is striking because it reveals that religious worldviews provide but one mental model among others that humans might employ to explain events or behaviors in the world. Just because a person has learned a religious model of the world, however, does not mean that that person will employ that conceptual scheme to explain all events. In fact, recent studies by Lupfer and colleagues (Lupfer et al. 1996) revealed that devoutly religious people do not even employ religious explanations for most events and everyday behaviors; the research subjects made supernatural attributions only between 6 percent and 46 percent of the time for positive occurrences, and 1 percent and 10 percent of the time (invoking Satan as the cause) for negative occurrences. Thus, even by the most liberal of estimates, people seem to prefer natural explanations for events and behaviors to supernatural explanations.

Attribution theory research suggests that instead of merely learning religion and then thinking religiously, humans instead run through the mental models available to them for the purpose of finding one that seems to work best. This widely used cognitive strategy has been termed "God-in-the-gaps reasoning" because humans seem to employ religious concepts when naturalistic explanations don't suffice.

While very useful for showing that religious ideas are but one of the "multiple sufficient schemata" (Kelly 1972) humans employ for cognitive tasks, attribution theories have a significant flaw: they don't explain why people employ nonnatural concepts at all. That religious explanations are employed across cultures raises the question of why so many people find them appealing. Fortunately, an answer to this problem has been offered. The work of such scholars as Thomas Lawson, Robert N. McCauley, Stewart Guthrie, Pascal Boyer, Harvey Whitehouse, and Justin Barrett (among others) has generated a significant body of knowledge about the cognitive origins of religious behavior that provides answers to why humans across cultures and epochs entertain and employ religious concepts.

The Ritual Form Hypothesis

The first book published on the cognitive science of religion was Lawson and McCauley's (1990) *Rethinking Religion: Connecting Cognition and Culture*. Inspired by Chomsky's competence theory of generative grammar (discussed earlier), they argued that participants in religious rituals possessed competency in their understanding of ritual form. Like Chomsky, they traced this tacit knowledge to the constraints of cognition. The foundation of their theory, which they have recently expanded to a "ritual form hypothesis" (McCauley & Lawson 2002), is the argument that human beings possess as part of their cognitive architecture an "action-representation-system" that informs our judgments about actions, events, and happenings in the world. The basic "theory" we have about actions is that there are occasions in which an actor performs an action on a patient (either a person or an object) or an action is performed on a patient.

ACTOR → ACTION → PATIENT

Examples are not hard to generate. "You drank wine." "John washed the car." "Brenda combed her hair."

What is important about how we represent actions is what is tacitly understood. Notice in the preceding examples what sorts of things are capable of being the doer: only "agents." That is, only things that have "intentionality." I did not say, because it is quite weird, "Wine drank you." "The car washed John." "The hair combed Brenda." All of these action representations are weird because in each an object is represented as an agent, which breaks the rules of cognition.

What would be even weirder would be "Washed the car John"; "Combed her hair Brenda"; "Drank wine you"; and the weirdest yet, "Washed John car the" or "Combed Brenda hair her." You probably just sense that something is wrong with these "sentences" (or that something is wrong with me, the author). That is an important feeling because it reveals that humans have a sense of "well-formedness" of actions (McCauley & Lawson 2002).

Now, what does this have to do with religious rituals? Well, take this example: The priest baptizes the baby. First, notice that the action itself has to follow certain rules (agent–action). Second, notice that it is a "well-formed" action. Third, notice that, in terms of the action-representation-system, the action "The priest baptized the baby" is the same as "The man poured water on the baby." So what makes a religious ritual different from an ordinary action? What makes baptism different from just pouring water, since they are the same action?

Religious rituals are different from ordinary actions insofar as the way they are represented cognitively includes another "layer" of representation—a symbolic layer—on top of the general action represented. The man (who is a priest) pours water on the baby. By virtue of the fact that the man doing the action is a priest, and he is performing the action in the context of a religious ceremony, the action being performed becomes "religious."

Of course, this leads to another question. What makes a representation (e.g., "man") a religious representation (e.g., "priest")? A religious representation is a representation that postulates the existence of superhuman agents. These things/beings are superhuman insofar as they are like us in many ways (they think, have emotions, etc.) but not like us in many other ways (they're invisible, have extraordinary powers, etc.). Most important, they are postulated as agents. This means that, by the rules of the action-representation-system, they can do things. They can act on us and on the world around us.

So let's get back to the priest. What makes a priest different (i.e., special) from an ordinary man that allows him to perform certain kinds of religious rituals that nonpriests cannot perform? The priest is special because a superhuman agent made him special through a previous ritual. Clergy members get their specialness from the superhuman agents who blessed them with it.

Consider what makes a priest a priest. A priest is an ordinary man who undergoes ordination/initiation into the clergy ranks of a religious system. Who ordains priests? Other priests. Who ordains those priests? Other priests, of course. Who ordained those priests? Other priests, of course. Through a process that Christian theologians call "apostolic succession," a clergy member is endowed with special power through a system of cumulative ordinations that goes all the way back to the very first ritual that was performed by the superhuman agent (God in the Christian system). If you know Christian history, you know that Jesus (i.e., God, according to the Christian Creeds) ordained Peter as the first bishop. Now every Catholic priest has special powers because of his ordination line. As I will show in chapter 5, the same general principle applies in Buddhism, and as it turns out, this principle of ordination applies in seemingly all religious traditions.

Lawson and McCauley's theory shows that the cognitive constraints on the representation of action result in religious rituals taking two (structural) forms: human actors doing things to gods (e.g., making sacrificial offerings), or gods doing things to patients via ritual officiates like priests (e.g., ordaining priests). Furthermore, in the most recent version of their theory, McCauley and Lawson (2002) point out that a ritual's form is accompanied by predictable levels of emotional and sensual stimulation, which they term "sensory pageantry." And those rituals in which human actors do things to gods, rituals they term "special patient rituals," are rituals that (can) get repeated relatively often, whereas those rituals in which the gods perform actions (via a ritual officiate) on patients, which they term "special agent rituals," occur usually only once in a person's lifetime.

Since special agent rituals are only performed once, these rituals tend to be surrounded with relatively high levels of sensory pageantry. Consider the fanfare with which weddings, baptisms, and initiations are celebrated, compared with the relative simplicity of making an offering to the gods at a shrine. Thus, according to tenets of the ritual form hypothesis, empirical predictions can be made about the repeatability and accompanying level of sensory pageantry based on any given ritual's structural form.

The ritual form hypothesis provides researchers with a means to explain the cognitive constraints of religious ritual form. Other cognitive scientists of religion, however, have explored the cognitive foundations of religious ideas. The work of scholars like Stewart Guthrie and Pascal Boyer supplements the work of McCauley and Lawson by providing explanations of the cognitive constraints on religious thoughts.

Hyperactive Agency Detection Device

After Lawson and McCauley's publication of *Rethinking Religion*, the next important book to be published in the cognitive science of religion was Guthrie's *Faces in the Clouds* (1993). Guthrie's work explored the phenomenon of anthropomorphism, in which humans attribute human characteristics (e.g., agency) to nonhuman things. According to Guthrie, "from voices in the wind, to Mickey Mouse, to Earth as Gaia" anthropomorphism is an involuntary universal feature of perception and the basis for religious thought (1993, pp. vii–viii).

What is anthropomorphism exactly? Think of this. You wake up in the middle of the night and feel thirsty. So you venture cautiously down the stairs toward the kitchen. Your eyes have yet to adjust to the darkness, and just as you reach the bottom and begin to turn the corner, you catch out of the corner of your eye something that moves. You jump. Your heart begins to race. Your senses are on high alert. You squint hard to make sense of the figure. Finally, it comes into focus . . . it's the coat tree in the corner.

Experiences in which we attribute agency to nonagents happen all the time. In fact, argues Guthrie, we are overly sensitive to the existence of agency in our world, so much so that we often misattribute agency where none is present. However, we rarely mistakes agents for nonagents. Why not?

Well, imagine yourself in the forest. You notice something on your left that is big, brown, and round. You turn immediately to detect what's there. Your heart starts pumping. Your anxiety level goes up. It's as big as you, and seems to be standing upright.

Could it be a bear? You become more scared; bears are dangerous. On second glance, though, to your relief you realize that it was just a big rock.

Now, imagine another scenario. You see another big, brown object as tall as you ahead on your right. Your immediately become anxious again because you don't instinctively think "Uh oh. That's a rock!" You think it's a bear. In fact, you'll keep thinking every object in your peripheral field of vision is something out to get you. Yet, according to Guthrie, not a single person in the world would ever mistake a bear for a rock. Rocks are mistaken for animals all the time, but we never mistake animals for rocks.

This is more than just an interesting anecdote, according to Guthrie. He argues that the instinct to anthropomorphize is an adaptive feature of human cognition. The reason for why we overattribute agency in our world is because it is advantageous to do so. Mistaking a rock for a bear is a little scary (and a little embarrassing, maybe) but to commonly mistake bears for rocks would be deadly. Thus it is our good fortune to have a "hyperactive agency detection device" (J. L. Barrett 2000). Of course the implication in Guthrie's theory is that anthropomorphism is a cognitive error. However, we shouldn't be embarrassed for making attribution errors; doing so is natural.

How does this relate to religion? Well, if anthropomorphism is the attribution of agency onto the world (often where none actually exists) and religion involves the attribution of agents in the world (often none are actually seen to exist), then religion is a form of anthropomorphism. Religion involves the attribution of agency onto the world: the gods caused me to win the lottery; demons made me do it; ghosts haunt the house; angels saved my life; there's a devil in that blue dress; the goddess killed the dinosaurs. Humans are prone to thinking religious thoughts because religious thoughts make convincing use of our natural proclivity to anthropomorphize.

Counterintuitiveness and Cognitive Optimum

You might be thinking to yourself by now, "Okay. I can see that we do all these things naturally. I admit, with some hesitation, that these things all influence religion in some way or another. What I

can't figure out, though, is where does all of this come from?"
Enter Pascal Boyer's theories of counterintuitiveness and cognitive
optimum.

Whereas Lawson and McCauley, and Guthrie, have put forth
very powerful theories of religious behavior, Boyer's work has
supplemented those theories with a catalogue of ideas that are
central to human cognition and that directly influence religious
thinking. Boyer has shown that religious concepts are constrained
cognitively by intuitions we have about the world and its workings.

Perform this thought experiment. Close your eyes. Think of
walking along a beautiful sandy beach. Think of the soft white
sand underneath your feet. Think of the ocean's waves rolling
gently over your toes. Think of a sleek dolphin jumping out of
the water just off the shore. Think of a young child building a
castle in the sand. Think of the sun setting at the end of the day.

That was pretty easy, right? You might say that it was pleasant.
Yet had I provided another representation for you to imagine,
your reaction would have been quite different. Try this.

Think of yourself on a beach with laughing sand. Think of the
dolphin building a castle on the beach. Think of the setting sun
saying, "Good night. See you tomorrow at sunrise."

How do these representations make you feel? Not "right," I
suspect, because they violate intuitions about what the world is
like and how it is supposed to work. Dolphins are supposed to
jump out of water, not build sand castles. The beach is not supposed to laugh, and of course the sun is not supposed to talk.

How do you know all of this? Did you learn it from your culture? It is possible that someone sat you down at some point in
your life and explicitly told you that dolphins don't build sand
castles, that the beach doesn't laugh, and that the sun does not
talk. That's possible, but unlikely. So how do you know that stuff?
You know it, Boyer points out, because human cognition provides
us with an intuitive ontology that gives us a sense of what the
world is like.

Importantly, our intuitive ontology is rule governed. What does
this mean? It means that while humans are not genetically predetermined to think only some thoughts and not others (nothing in
your genetic package predetermined that you would think about
talking suns and castle-building dolphins!) but your intuitive on-

tology governs thought in such a way that some thoughts are more "natural" than others. In this way, your intuitive ontology allows you to make sense of what's going on in the world.

The examples in my second thought experiment (laughing beaches, talking sun) were instructive because those representations violated your expectations about the world. Expectation-violations tend to cause a reaction of surprise, and violations of intuitive ontological kinds (suns, beaches, dolphins, etc.) are the basis of religious representations. How is it possible to get religious ideas from intuitive ontology?

Clearly religious representations violate the expectations of our intuitive ontology. Just think of what gods are like: they are "superhuman," in the sense that they possess many of the same postulated qualities as humans but with important violations. For example, gods are typically thought of as humanlike beings that live somewhere, have minds, can hear you, see you, talk to you (if they choose), do stuff to you (if they choose), get mad, are jealous, can be made happy, and on and on and on. Yet don't be fooled by the humanlike qualities of gods, because gods are quite different from us in other ways. Gods typically don't die. They are invisible. They know the future before it happens. They can see everywhere all at once. They don't eat, but they don't get hungry. They can go in and out of your body. They can fly, go through walls undetected, and many of them are believed to have existed since the beginning of time.

However, religious representations don't just randomly violate our expectations about the world. Instead, according to Boyer, religious representations either breech default expectations about natural kinds or they transfer expectations from one domain to another. We have this capacity because the number of things in the world presumed by our intuitive ontology is very small. Humans differentiate natural kinds into five types of things:

1. Natural objects (e.g., rocks)
2. Artificial (i.e., made by humans) objects (e.g., chairs)
3. Plants (e.g., flowers)
4. Animals (e.g., dogs)
5. Humans

Importantly, each natural kind is presumed to have essential features that distinguish it from the other things. Generally, things possess more complex features the farther they are along the ontological spectrum (from one to five). Natural and artificial objects are nonliving things. As such, we know that they don't move by their own volition (i.e., they have to be physically pushed, or "launched," by something). Natural and artificial objects don't grow. They don't need food. They aren't born. They don't die. Plants, however, are living things (albeit "simple"). They grow. They need some kind of food and water to live. They die. And so on. More complicated still, animals are living things that have volition. They grow, die, need food and water, are born, and they can think (however primitively).

Finally, humans are special kinds of animals. Humans not only have volition, they in fact have (more highly developed) minds. Representing humans as "animals with fancy minds" is an important feature of our intuitive ontology, because that capacity enables us to live (fairly) successfully in groups. Having a "theory of mind" or "folk psychology" (i.e., the ability to represent what other people think, know, desire, feel, etc.) allows us to communicate, to build trusting relationships, to detect liars and cheats, and so forth. Amazingly, humans are able to know what each other are thinking (Baron-Cohen 1995; Boyer 1994; Pinker 1997).

Now, recall the supernatural kinds of representations that we call religious: gods that don't die; goddesses that are jealous; demons that don't have to eat; ghosts that are invisible; spirits that can foretell the future. What do they all share in common? These representations are *counterintuitive;* they are nonnatural but learnable (Boyer 1994).

But why are representations that violate expectations appealing? One would think that only natural representations would make sense to us. However, that is not really the case. As it turns out, humans are quite interested in nonnatural representations. In fact nonnatural representations, because they are surprising, are quite easy to entertain and quite easy to remember. It seems that people find "weird" (by the standards of ontology) facts interesting. Consider the following story.

> Tim Smith is fourteen years old. He walks home every day from school, which is located in a suburb just outside of a large city. Tim's walk takes longer than most teenagers' because he has no legs. The walk itself is approximately one mile long, and it takes Tim about four days to complete it. Today, he is hoping to make

his journey safely because last week a pink dragon bit him—and his mother didn't like that much at all because it made Tim late for dinner.

By my count, there are about seventeen facts in this story. Yet were I to ask you to recall them, you would probably remember four parts of the story best:

1. Tim has no legs.
2. One mile takes four days to complete.
3. A pink dragon bit Tim
4. Tim's mother was angry that he missed dinner, but showed no surprise that a pink dragon bit him.

Compared to these parts of the story, other facts will be less reliably recalled. You might not even remember some facts at all (e.g., that the suburb is outside a large city).

What exactly does this have to do with religion? If you think back to Sperber's account of what constitutes a public representation, the point should become clear. One of the reasons why religious ideas have such widespread appeal is that they are interesting (i.e., attention grabbing), and because they are interesting they have a great chance of being transmitted successfully. They achieve a cognitive optimum.

Of these, the commonly recurring representations are those that involve agency, probably because of the representational tendencies of the hyperactive agency detection device. Thus, the kinds of (supernatural) things that populate religious systems tend to be agents, either humans with breech violations or objects, plants, or animals with transferred human-expectations (e.g., talking rocks, walking trees, trickster animals, etc.) So when someone tells a child that little Rover, the family puppy, is in heaven after being hit by a car, the idea is powerful. It is an idea that is cognitively optimal.

Modes of Religiosity

Boyer's theories of counterintuitiveness and cognitive optimum provide a robust account of why religious ideas get transmitted successfully in human cultures. However, Harvey Whitehouse has argued that religious concepts can be successfully transmitted in more than one way. According to Whitehouse, ethnographic evidence reveals two "modes" of religiosity, each with different means of transmitting religious ideas (Whitehouse 1995, 2000). Whitehouse has argued that religions tend to diverge into either a "doctrinal" or an "imagistic" mode of religiosity because of the psychological dynamics of memory and motivation that underlie the spread of concepts.

Whitehouse's arguments rest on the assumption that religious concepts are not equal in their representational complexity. Some are maximally counterintuitive (e.g., the Christian God is formless yet omnipresent) whereas others are minimally counterintuitive (e.g., recently deceased ancestors can hear prayers). Due to their cognitive complexity, maximally counterintuitive concepts require special kinds of mechanisms for successful transmission, and Whitehouse has offered an account of how each mode provides such mechanisms. According to Whitehouse, the transmission of religious concepts in each mode differs by "style of codification," and he has identified thirteen variables for successful transmission in each mode (Whitehouse 1995, 2000).

Maximally counterintuitive concepts are transmitted in the doctrinal mode through frequent repetition and frequent performance of ritual actions. Due to this routinization, the religious knowledge available to both leaders and laity is stored in semantic memory (i.e., as a body of "general knowledge") that has become somewhat rigidly standardized. Emphasis on the medium of language (e.g., sermons and other specialized forms of oratory, as well as on the written word) facilitates rapid and efficient spread of such traditions across large territories. In contrast, in traditions dominated by the imagistic mode, religious thinking depends more on processes of spontaneous exegetical reflection than on oral transmission. In addition, low-frequency, high-arousal rituals trigger enduring episodic memory. This not only triggers particular modalities of religious thinking and revelation but also produces special patterns of spread and group formation, with the result that such traditions are either small-scale and localized or regionally fragmented.

But each mode has certain vulnerabilities too. Survival of maximally counterintuitive concepts in the doctrinal mode depends on effective policing by a religious hierarchy. If the leaders pay insufficient attention to training and "drilling" their followers, or if they fail to monitor and police the orthodoxy, people will tend to simplify the official teachings so as to produce more minimally counterintuitive or frankly intuitive versions. Whitehouse (2004) refers to this as the "cognitive optimum effect." On the other hand, if the leaders become too fanatical about the teaching and policing of their orthodoxy and the disciplines of worship and study become too severe and demanding, people may become frustrated and demoralized, a situation that Whitehouse (2000) refers to as the "tedium effect." Although the imagistic mode lacks these sorts of internal contradictions, it is often subject to suppression by the leaders of more routinized orthodoxies. Especially in periods of imperialistic iconoclasm, to which most traditions operating in the doctrinal mode are liable to succumb at one time or another, the imagistic mode may come under great pressure to abandon or sanitize its more colorful or high-arousal practices.

However, both modes of religiosity, once established, can be very robust historically. In fact, Whitehouse argues that they often operate very effectively in tandem, within a single tradition. For example, where a doctrinal mode of operation is counterbalanced by imagistic traditions, as Whitehouse observed in certain new religious movements in Melanesia, the twin problems of the doctrinal mode, namely under- and overpolicing, can be avoided. What's important about Whitehouse's theory for my purpose here is that while the style of codification in either mode results in successful transmission of religious concepts, neither mode determines that religious participants will always employ the same concepts. When official (centralized) theological concepts are not sufficiently policed in the doctrinal mode, participants' representations are likely to degenerate into minimally counterintuitive concepts that come to them more naturally. And the dynamics of spontaneous exegetical reflection in the imagistic mode can result in significant variation in beliefs and practices.

Theological Correctness: What People Really Think

The works of Sperber, Lawson and McCauley, Guthrie, Boyer, and Whitehouse have collectively established a cognitive "paradigm of research" (Kuhn 1970) in the study of religion. Paradigms provide scholars with foundational assumptions about a given object of study that guide research. The collective theories of these scholars have explained why people employ "supernatural" concepts in their "natural" traffic with the world. As important, however, paradigmatic works also point to new avenues of research. In this regard, exciting research into the actual employment of religious concepts in everyday thinking has been undertaken by a host of other scholars in the last few years (Andresen 2001; Antonnen & Pyysiäinen 2002; Atran 2002; Barnes 2001; Mithen 1996; Pyysiäinen 2001; Rosengren, Johnson, & Harris 2000). Of the growing body of research, Justin Barrett's research on "theological correctness" merits the most attention here.

If you think about all of the cognitive scientists' claims together, something interesting emerges. Sperber pointed out that because ideas spread in a given population, they are constantly undergoing transformation: when people make their representations public, and then when recipients of the representation hear and process them. In other words, you can't step into the same river twice; representations are always changing.

Yet some ideas achieve a cognitive optimum and do become transmitted successfully. Just think of some such representations: nursery rhymes ("Humpty Dumpty sat on a wall . . ."), jingles and popular songs ("Yankee Doodle went to town / riding on a pony / stuck a feather in his hat and . . ."), memorable poems ("Two roads diverged in a wood . . ."), and so on. Such public representations are especially transmittable. Generations of Americans learn, memorize, and retell these kinds of representations. They become classics.

Certain religious representations spread in the same way. I can still sing "Jesus Loves Me . . . this I know . . . for the Bible tells me so . . ." I can also remember certain passages from the Bible ("God said, 'Let there be light,' and there was light."), certain prayers ("Now I lay me down to sleep, I pray the Lord my soul to keep . . ."), and so forth. Theological doctrines are also committed to memory ("We believe in the Father, and the Son, and in the Holy Spirit . . ."). So which is it? Do ideas constantly change or do they stay the same (i.e., become "traditional")? The answer is . . . both.

Barrett suggests that we think of religious ideas as "lying on a continuum of abstractness or cognitive complexity" because he noticed during narrative recall experiments that people sometimes generate representations that contradict what they profess to believe (J. L. Barrett 1999, p. 325). When asked traditional theological questions (e.g., "Do you believe God is all-knowing and all-powerful?"), people provide theologically correct answers, probably those they've memorized. Yet, when asked to recall short narratives they had read that included passages about faith-specific deities, respondents in research experiments tended to systematically misremember the stories in such a way that revealed their tendencies toward theological correctness. When participants retold the stories they had read, they infused the narratives with deity characteristics that were not part of the original narrative. For example, though professing to believe that God can do all things at one time, participants in the experiments represented God as, like humans, having to complete one task before attending to another. In the minds of the research participants, God answers one prayer in one part of the world and then moves on to the next, even though, theologically, He can do all things at once. Such technically theologically incorrect representations revealed that people possess tacit presumptions about superhuman agency that are not necessarily in line with official theological doctrines (J. L. Barrett 1999, 2001; Barrett & Keil 1998; Barrett & Nyhof 2001).

Obviously, this body of research supports the paradigmatic assumption in the cognitive science of religion that the religious ideas are constrained by ordinary cognition. However, Barrett's research shows that the limited processing constraints of the mind-brain results in humans possessing multiple levels of representation. Humans can know one thing in one context but represent it differently (even contradict their deeply held "beliefs") in another context, if the context demands generating rapid, easy-to-recall or infer representations. This finding in turn advances the hypotheses of the attribution theorists as well. Even when humans employ religious concepts, the religious concepts they generate might be more consistent with folk knowledge than with official theology. Sorry, clergy, but theological ideas simply do not determine, per se, how or what people think.

Cognitive theories provide scholars with a powerful set of tools to analyze religion. The scholars mentioned in this chapter have established a paradigm within which other scholars can begin to explain interesting features of human behavior. By showing how religious concepts are similar across cultures and yet undergo significant change from person to person, we can begin to make sense of religious behavior. I can now begin to explain some particular instances of theological incorrectness. The next three chapters explore three case studies of theological incorrectness involving two different religious systems in two different cultures: Theravada Buddhism in Southeast Asia, Christianity in colonial America, and luck beliefs in both cultures.

CHAPTER FOUR

※

BUDDHA NATURE

Superhuman agents are a force to be reckoned with; at least that's what religion seems to be about. Religion involves doing rituals and other sorts of activities that are predicated on presumptions about what kind of beings superhuman agents are. In this sense, what religious people do tends to follow from what they think (or what someone in their religious system tells them to think). Religious behavior turns on presumptions that superhuman agents exist and we ought to do what they want us to do (or not do, as the case may be).

While religious thought involves the presumption that superhuman agents exist, theology involves postulations about those agents. This dual feature of religion seems to apply across the board: religious systems across cultures contain theological postulations about such issues as our cosmological origins, suffering and salvation, the meaning of life, human destiny, and so on, as well as "folk" religious presumptions such as that worshiping superhuman agents can bring one practical benefits like healing, good fortune, and immortality. Yet anyone who is familiar with the various religions of the world is aware that one religious system, Theravada Buddhism of South and Southeast Asia, seems to challenge this assumption and therefore our understanding of religion. Theravada Buddhism is a very widespread and purportedly nontheistic religion that originated in India around twenty-five hundred years ago and then spread throughout South Asia, where it is still practiced widely today (Gombrich 1988; Robinson & Johnson 1982). This raises an issue. If Theravada Buddhism is a successfully transmitted nontheistic religion, then religion cannot be simply about super-human agents. And if there is a religion that is significantly unlike the rest, then we might not be able to compare religions at all. Thus, before we can proceed to any other discussions about religion, we have to settle the question of what constitutes "religion," or else our discussion will be imprecise and incoherent.

Metatheory and the Category of Religion

Fortunately, enough work has been done on issues related to this problem that solutions are available. One approach is known as "metatheoretical" because it involves addressing theories of theory. Metatheory requires asking the question "What theory supports what counts as a category?" The category in question here happens to be "religion," but the same question could apply to any other category like "umbrella" or "zebra." With little reflection, what things like religions and umbrellas and zebras are seems to be self-evident. An umbrella is something that keeps the rain (or sun) off of us. To be precise, an umbrella is "a collapsible shade for protection against weather consisting of fabric stretched over hinged ribs radiating from a central pole." On the other hand, a zebra is a striped horse. Or, to be precise, it is "any of several fleet African mammals (genus *Equus burchelli, E. grevyi,* and *E. zebra*) related to the horse but distinctively and conspicuously patterned in the stripes of black or dark brown and white or buff." At least that's what my dictionary says (*Merriam-Webster's Tenth Collegiate Dictionary* 2002).

However, what if the umbrella material that is stretched over the hinged ribs radiating from a central pole is thin rubber and not fabric? Would it still be an umbrella? What if the zebra had red and green stripes instead of black or dark brown and white or buff? Would it still be a zebra?

What if the umbrella had no fabric (or thin rubber) at all to protect you from the elements but instead was just a metal pole with some hinged ribs attached? Would it still be an umbrella? What if the zebra had no stripes at all? Would it still be a zebra?

Your instinctive answers to these questions are probably yes to the first two but no to the last two. Why? The classical definition of what makes a thing a thing is that it has to fulfill "necessary and sufficient conditions." In other words, a thing is a thing if and only if it has certain properties, like protective fabric in the case of the umbrella and stripes in the case of zebras. This way of defining a thing can be quite useful, for scientists especially. Classical definitions allow us to say with precision, for example, that a collection of thin metal poles does not constitute an umbrella and a horse without stripes does not constitute a zebra.

However, this classical way of defining objects has a serious limitation. Although it works well for scientific classification, it is not quite as useful for informal thinking. Consider how humans represent things like "birds" and "persons." What makes a bird a bird? The intuitive way we represent birds is as animals that can fly. Yet penguins, which, classically defined, are birds, cannot fly. Furthermore, consider what makes a person a person. A person is . . . well, we just seem to "know" what a person is. What is an African American? Well, we just seem to know what an African American is. Or do we? Scientists have significant trouble identifying any biological marker of race, but it is common for humans to represent humans as belonging to one race or another nevertheless (Hirschfeld 1996).

Cognitive scientists have discovered that humans categorize objects in the world through the use of prototypes. In our daily lives we do not always employ the classical way of defining things that philosophers and scientists revere. Rather, we use (among other strategies) prototypical thinking, because that way of categorizing the world's components is economical; it does not require the laborious (and often limiting) task of identifying the exact properties that define an object. In prototypical thinking, we infer, or "theorize" if you will, from a prototypical image of one thing, whether or not and in what sorts of ways another thing is like that prototypical thing. Consider again the case of "bird." If we intuitively defined birds in such a way as to exclude "flies" as an essential (in this case, functional) property, then the definition would seem not to capture what we tend to think of as what a bird is. A prototypical definition, in contrast, captures a rich "feel" for what a thing is. A robin, for example, is a good prototype of a bird, and so in our everyday thinking we are likely to tacitly compare all birds against this prototype (at least in our sociocultural context). Thus any given bird in question is categorized as "more or less" like a robin . . . and therefore "more or less" a bird.

A penguin is a bird, but "less so" than say a parakeet or a jay. Thus, prototypical thinking leads us away from the "either-or" distinction of classical definitions in favor of a "more-or-less" kind of thinking that is very useful for everyday situations (Medin 1998).

In this regard, religion might be more fruitfully construed prototypically than classically. A religion involves postulations and presumptions that superhuman agents exist, and any religious system that includes such features counts, in most people's minds, as more like a religion than one that does not (note that definitions follow from theories). Thus, if Buddhism does not include such features, it could still be considered a religion (as a penguin can be considered a bird), though a peculiar one by comparison. This is a very useful way of thinking about religion because it is much more in line with human beings' actual cognition than classical definitions tend to be.

Having said that makes it easier to evaluate whether Theravada Buddhism is more or less a "real" (i.e., prototypical) religion. As is turns out, it most certainly is. Despite the existence of strands of nontheism in Theravada theology, ethnographic data collected in Theravada cultures reveals that Theravada Buddhism is very much like other prototypical religious systems because of the widespread representation of the Buddha as a superhuman agent. Despite what many books written for a Western audience say about Buddhism, Buddhists are quite religious.

Buddhism by the Books

In the image that has been circulating in the Western world for some time, Buddhism is presented as an austere, highly philosophical wisdom tradition that relies not on gods and superstitions but rather on keen mental and ethical skills that can be honed by any spiritually self-reliant individual (e.g., Rahula 1959). In this view, the Buddha is represented as "just a man" and Buddhism therefore as not a religion per se but rather something like a system of ethics or a psychological "way of life." As such Buddhism has served over the years as a test case for scholarly definitions of religion (B. C. Wilson 1999).

Unfortunately, that image does not represent Theravada Buddhism as it is actually practiced in most parts of the world. In reality, Theravada Buddhists are not very different from practitioners of other religions. They too conceptualize their central figure (i.e., the Buddha) as a superhuman agent, and they worship him (and other superhuman agents) in hopes of achieving practical benefits. Yet the counterimage persists in the West. Why is this so? There are historical reasons.

The form of Buddhism that most Westerners know is actually a form of what one scholar has called "Buddhist modernism" and is based on narrow readings of the religion's theological postulations that were popularized during the nineteenth century in South Asia, primarily in Sri Lanka, in large measure as a response to colonialism. This movement has been dubbed "modernism" because, having begun among urban, Western-educated, middle-class reformers, it mirrored the kinds of modernist movements found throughout Europe at that time (Bechert 1966, 1967, 1973).

The generation of Buddhist modernism came at the hands of educated reformers who felt that the best way to battle the colonizing Christians (and therefore colonialism by extension) was to revive and reassert the philosophical aspects of ancient Buddhist teachings. Like reformers in Europe, they used modern methods to do so. This revived, reformed version of Buddhism was spread by means of mass education via public sermons and the use of the printing press for the publication and distribution of Buddhist materials. Christians had established missionary schools throughout Sri Lanka during the latter stages of the colonial period, and an English-based education was a popular strategy for upward mobility among the middle class. In response, Buddhist reformers fought the "Anglicization" of their society by offering Buddhist social alternatives. They created their own Buddhist schools for the teaching of both secular subjects and of modernist Buddhism to the masses, who were, the reformers believed, insufficiently equipped to resist British colonialism. Interestingly, an American, Henry Steele Olcott, and a few other Westerners who had become interested in Buddhism and native resistance to the British Christians, assisted them in their endeavors. Olcott helped create a Buddhist catechism to ensure a "proper" Buddhist education for the masses of Singhalese Buddhists. Lay groups like the Young Men's Buddhist Association were also formed to rival their Christian counterparts' organizations and provide Buddhist-based social activities and for networking (Bond 1988; Gombrich & Obeyesekere 1988; Malalgoda 1976; Prothero 1995).

These revivalists also began to preach publicly their version of Buddhism, which was mined from scriptural passages that were highly philosophical in orientation. They often challenged—and defeated, in the eyes of many natives—the Christian missionaries in public debates through the use of reasoned and rational arguments supported by textual evidence from the Pali Buddhist canon, the *Tripitika*. Their message was that Buddhism was superior to Christianity because the Buddha was a noble philosopher who taught an empirically verifiable modern philosophy that emphasized the role of individual effort over dependence on deities for salvation. The Buddhist reformers dubbed Christianity, by contrast, as superstitious and not in line with science and the modern world.

The education of the masses via Buddhist schools, lay organizations, and public debates was augmented by the widespread distribution of Buddhist philosophical scriptures. The Buddhist activists purchased printing presses and began distributing vernacular versions of the Buddhist teachings throughout Sri Lanka. In addition to the Pali scriptures, they wrote commentarial Buddhist tracts that served their reformist agenda—to awaken the masses out of their superstitious and empty rituals (i.e., traditional devotional practices).

The result of their efforts was the creation of a form of Buddhism that reflected not the beliefs and values of indigenous Buddhists but rather that of post-Enlightenment Protestant Christianity. Buddhist modernism emphasized individual choice, explicitly criticized popular practices, rejected the traditional authority of the sangha (community of monks) as preservers of the *dharma* (Buddhist doctrine), and linked religion with nationalist concerns. As such, leading scholars of Theravada later dubbed this modernist tradition "Protestant Buddhism" (Gombrich & Obeyesekere 1988; Tambiah 1992). The most famous Protestant Buddhists of this time were Anagarika Dharmapala, a Singhalese layman who lived like a monk and worked for social change by putting modernist principles into action, and Olcott, in whose memory contemporary Singhalese celebrate a national holiday (Gombrich & Obeyesekere 1988; Prothero 1995).

Thus, nineteenth-century intellectuals, both Asian and Western, crafted this version of Buddhism to serve anticolonial political agendas. These intellectuals presented Buddhism as a religion for the modern world because it was seen to be nontheistic and therefore in line with modern science. According to this view, the Buddha merely taught metaphysical and ethical laws of the universe that were empirically available to all through reasonable and rational study of and reflection on the dharma or through personal insights achieved in meditation (this feature of Buddhism might sound familiar). Of course Buddhist devotional practices has long centered on worship of the Buddha and other forms of superhuman agency including other Buddhas, *arhants* ("perfected monks"), relics, *stupas* (burial grounds containing relics), icons, and even thaumaturgical texts (Lopez 1995a; Spiro 1970; Swearer 1995). Popular devotional practices were dismissed as superstitious, non-Buddhist, and in the cases of the northern schools of Buddhism— Mahayana, Vajrayana, and Tantra—Hinduized corruptions of the true dharma (believed to be preserved in the Pali canon as Christian truth was preserved in the Bible).

Contemporary scholars have pointed out that this image not only misrepresented the tradition as it was practiced historically but also was actually perpetuated by "Orientalist" (Said 1979) intellectuals in colonialist contexts, and was sustained by narrow readings of a small number of selectively edited texts found in the *Tripitika* (texts that, Schopen [1997] has pointed out, were themselves the edited products of ideal-minded monks). Beginning in the 1960s, the anthropologists and historians of religion Melford Spiro, Stanley Tambiah, Richard Gombrich, Gananath Obeyesekere, and others began to correct this interpretation of Buddhism by showing that Buddhism as practiced "on the ground" possessed a rich religious, that is, devotional, dimension. They showed that Buddhist modernists had focused only on the "ought" of Buddhism (a common result of any study of religion based on theological scriptures) at the expense of the "is." Buddhism on the ground consists of copious merit-making rituals like *puja* (rituals of devotion performed to the Buddha and other superhuman agents), *dana* (sacrificial giving to monks and other members of the Buddhism community), pilgrimage, and so forth. And these practices were fully institutionalized in cults of stupas, icons, saints, and more.

Nancy Falk, in her (1972) dissertation on the cult of relics in Buddhism, further showed that the modernists' image of the Buddha—as "just a man"—misrepresented what kind of being Buddhists actually understood the Buddha to be. According to modernist textual readings, the Buddha was not only "just a man" during his life but also was now "unavailable" to Buddhists because at his death he achieved *parinirvana*, or complete extinction from rebirth and *samsara* ("existence"). Falk showed instead that the supposedly absent Buddha is believed to be present in "sacred traces" like relics, statues, icons, and so on.

More recent scholarship has confirmed Falk's hypothesis. Scholars have collected numerous popular stories that depict the Buddha as having many of the characteristics of deities in other religions. He is variously depicted as having the thirty-two (biological) marks of a deity, as being omniscient, as being omnipotent, as being capable of performing miracles, and so on (Dharmasena 1991; Premchit & Swearer 1998; Schober 1997). Furthermore, using archeological inscriptions and other epigraphical texts from early north Indian Buddhism, Gregory Schopen has shown that monks and nuns commonly performed the very same kinds of rituals as the laity. They donated gifts, contributed to the building of stupas, cared for deceased relatives, buried the dead at sacred locations, and so forth, in hopes of accumulating merit and thereby gaining powers like the ability to perform miracles and healings, to be reborn as a deity, or to cheat death altogether (Schopen 1997).

Thus, Buddhists are very "religious." Monks and laity alike are very much concerned with the same kinds of practical benefits that persons of other religions are. The issue of whether or not Theravada Buddhism is "really" a religion thus rests on a conflation of the "Great" traditions of Theravada (i.e., Buddhist modernism) and the "Little" traditions (i.e., Buddhism on the ground) (Southwold 1984). Yet, recognizing that Theravada Buddhism has two "traditions" begs the question of why there is a difference in the first place. If religion is the internalization of theology, there ought not to be a gap between official theology and actual beliefs/ practices. Thus, whence come the "Little" traditions?

Representing the Buddha

At the heart of the question about why Buddhists are "religious" if the Buddha taught nontheism is a more fundamental question about the nature of the Buddha. For example, how is it Buddhists simultaneously hold that the Buddha has achieved parinirvana and therefore has no existence and yet is still "present" to be worshiped? Fortunately, cognitive research suggests an answer. In fact, there are actually two answers to this question because the problem is actually based on two puzzles. The first puzzle is how can people represent dead persons as still being "alive" after death at all? The second puzzle is how can a person, dead or alive, be represented as being "present" in objects (e.g., relics) that are physically separate from his or her body?

An answer to the first question requires that we understand how human beings conceptualize death in general, because how human beings represent dead persons has much to do with the belief in the continuation of the Buddha despite his death and parinirvana (and all beliefs in an afterlife). The belief in the continuation of life after death is made possible by the cognitive capacity to represent objects as existing despite their apparent nonexistence (as indicated by their absence from our immediate perceptual field). One of the first psychologists to study this phenomenon scientifically was Jean Piaget, who called it the capacity for "object permanency" (Piaget 1926, 1954). Representing objects as existing permanently is so basic to our cognitive abilities that we often don't even notice that we do it, even though it is a quite remarkable feat. Consider this. You are sitting in the living room watching a movie with your spouse. In the middle of the movie, your spouse hits the pause button on the remote control and goes to the kitchen to make some popcorn. As she (or he) turns the corner of the doorway, she goes out of your sight. Yet you know that she still exists. She is, according to your mind, simply somewhere else. Furthermore, you know that popcorn, a popcorn popper, bowls, salt, and butter also exist, even though you have no direct perceptual evidence for this knowledge at your immediate disposal. So how do you know these things exist? Well, you don't, really. You presume that these things exist because you've "encoded" them, we'll say, in your memory. You "represent" these objects as existing, and once an object is represented as existing, you represent it as always existing somewhere in the world (e.g., in the kitchen cupboard). Thus, you can represent objects as existing because you have the capacity for "object permanency."

The capacity for object permanency suggests that the belief in afterlife is natural. Though still instructive, Piaget's theories have been fine-tuned in the past few years. One of the most interesting neo-Piagetian discoveries is that our supposed object permanency is actually even more sophisticated than Piaget proposed. Our capacity for object permanency is actually domain specific (Hirschfeld & Gelman 1994). We can conceptualize some kinds of things as existing outside of our perceptual domain, possibly forever, while we can postulate other things as actually ceasing to exist. Some things last forever. Others do not.

Think of this. Your spouse reenters the room with a big bowl of salty, buttery popcorn. Your presumptions were correct! All of those things did exist! Now, you restart the movie and dig in to the snack. After twenty minutes or so, you reach down and finish off the very last kernel of popcorn. To your appetite's dismay, the popcorn is gone.

In a different sense, however, the popcorn is not gone at all. One could argue plausibly that the popcorn simply exists in another form in your digestive system. Yet it is highly unlikely that many people would intuitively think of the popcorn as still existing, just existing in another form somewhere else. Of course, the popcorn is in your stomach. But in your stomach it is being broken down by your digestive system, and when it exits your body, it will look (and smell) nothing like it did going in your mouth. According to our everyday cognition, the popcorn has ceased to exist.

This view of the nonexistence of consumed popcorn should be rather uncontroversial. What about when a living thing, like a pet or a person, dies? Do we have the same ease in representing the living agent as ceasing to exist?

The psychologist Jesse Bering recently put this question to the test. In a clever set of experiments, he and a colleague presented elementary school children with a puppet show in which a mouse was eaten by an alligator (the experiment was performed in Florida, so the students were familiar with alligators). Before the alligator ate the mouse, the students were told that the mouse was having a very bad day. According to the story, the mouse had gotten lost and so had spent all day searching for its home. As such, the mouse was thirsty, hungry, and tired. Then, to make matters worse, the mouse happened on an alligator, which ate it for dinner. As a result, the mouse was no longer alive (Bering 2001).

Bering then asked a series of questions designed to unearth the children's intuitions about what was happening to the dead mouse. The questions were divided along domain-specific lines (biological, psychological, and epistemic). The first questions dealt with the domain of biology. The students were asked whether the mouse would, after having been killed by the alligator, eat dinner that night. Nearly all said no. Then they were asked if the mouse would sleep that night. Again, nearly all said no. Thus, according to indications from the experiment, biological functions such as eating and sleeping seem to cease on death in the minds of these children.

The next set of questions Bering posed to the children were psychological and epistemic, that is, were about what the mouse was thinking, feeling, and knowing. The students were asked if the mouse would be hungry that night, if the mouse would be tired that night, and if the mouse was mad at the alligator for eating (and thus killing) him. Astonishingly, many of the respondents, especially among the younger group (ages four to seven) responded yes. Thus, though the mouse's biological functions ceased on death, certain psychological and epistemic functions did not.

On the basis of these results, along with other research, Bering concluded that children could represent the cessation of biological (and by default physical) functions of an agent quite easily, but they have difficulty representing the cessation of psychological (and by extension epistemic) functions. This is important because in prototypical thinking, what makes an agent, like a mouse—or a human—an agent is that it has *psychological* abilities. In other words, the "essence" of a mouse (and a human) is its functioning mind.

Now consider that the etymology of the word "psyche," which today means "mind" but was originally the word for "soul." In nearly all cultures, afterlife is represented as being the place where souls (or some culturally specific equivalent) go. This fact seems to be explained by Bering's cognitive experiments. Humans believe in the continuation of a person's "essence," "spirit," or "soul" after death because our minds, which allow us to represent the existence of people and objects outside of our immediate perceptual field, have great difficulty in representing the cessation of the psychological existence of an agent. This means that humans presume that an "afterlife" exists because it is natural to do so (H. C. Barrett 1998, 2001; Barrett & Behne 2001; Bering 2001; Boyer 2001).

Now, recall the belief in the continued existence of the Buddha. As I said earlier, Buddhists are often taught that he is no longer around because he achieved parinirvana. If cognitive theories are correct, then the representation of the Buddha as dead but not gone would achieve a cognitive optimum (see chapter 3). In other words, Buddhists could learn the idea that the Buddha does not exist any longer in the "here and now" but also be capable of believing that he is actually still around somewhere. Further, from this we could predict that Buddhists would say in situations that require them to be theologically correct that the Buddha is in parinirvana yet in other situations treat him as if that were not the case. This is precisely what scholars have found during ethnographic observation in Buddhist cultures. Buddhists appear to have "split brains" because they simultaneously claim to believe in the Buddha's parinirvana yet presume that their prayers and offerings to him are efficacious because he is around to receive them (e.g., Gombrich & Obeyesekere 1988; Southwold 1984; Spiro 1970; Swearer 1995; Tambiah 1970, 1976, 1984).

Essences and Traces

As mentioned earlier, the Buddha is also represented as being present in sacred traces like icons, bodhi trees, amulets, relics housed in stupas, and other similar objects. While our inability to represent the cessation of psychological functions might explain the recurring belief in continuation of life after death in the form of spiritual essences, it does not explain why Buddhists (and many other religious people, for that matter) presume that objects can be imbued with superhuman agency. For this there must be an overlapping cognitive capacity.

The capacity that explains the phenomenon of sacred traces is related to what Boyer, drawing on the previous work of Rozin (1976) and Rozin, Haidt, and McCauley (1993), calls the cognitive "contagion system" (Boyer 2001). In this view, human beings have the cognitive ability to represent the transference of the essence of one object completely into another.

Consider this. You walk into your bedroom to go to sleep. You pull back the blankets to find to your surprise and disgust that your bed is infested with bugs. There are little creatures crawling everywhere . . . all over your mattress, your pillow, your sheets, and so forth. What would you do? Most likely, you would jump back and scream. Then you would set about disinfecting your bed thoroughly. You might even throw away the linens altogether (possibly the mattress, too).

Why would you go to such lengths? Wouldn't it suffice to simply remove the bugs? Probably not, because you would have a deep sense that the bed had become "infested" with the essence of the bugs (which is, to say the least, gross). Though the bugs can be removed, they have already done their damage because their essence has been, at least in our minds, transferred into the sheets, the blankets, the pillows, and the mattress. This is because human minds have some kind of contagion detection device (technically, a collection of devices) that represents the transference of an object's essence into another object on contact. Spiders, snakes, and other "creepies" are bad enough to see, but if one is crawling on you . . . (go ahead and image a spider crawling on your leg right now).

Studies in which subjects were presented with objects that had come into contact with defiled material reveal this tendency. One of the most telling experiments along these lines involved asking subjects to drink out of a glass that had once had feces as its contents. Despite thoroughly disinfecting the once defiled glass, most subjects balked at the experimenters' requests to drink out of it. Would you?

The contagion system seems to work both ways, however. Not only can objects be infected with bad essences but evidence from cultures worldwide suggests that objects can be imbued with positive essences as well. Religious people seemingly everywhere believe that the essence of a holy person can be transferred into an object, which can in turn be tapped for power. In the case of Theravada Buddhism, much of daily religious life consists of attending to objects that are believed to have special powers, often because they are associated with holy monks who themselves are considered to have special powers. The anthropologist Stanley Tambiah has noted a widespread cult of amulets in Thailand (and such cults exist in all Buddhist cultures), where people regularly buy amulets that have been blessed by monks who are believed to have extraordinary powers. Once purchased, one keeps the amulets physically near one's body for protection against evil and misfortune (Tambiah 1984). Similar phenomena have been documented in other religions in regions as disparate as China, Japan, Africa, Europe, and the United States (see Earhart 1993). Most likely, this phenomenon recurs worldwide.

Similarly, stupas and other sacred spaces where relics are housed are common sites where pilgrims trek to obtain spiritual (and by extension practical) benefits. The most famous site in Sri Lanka houses that which is believed to be an actual tooth of the Buddha. Not only do individuals seek to get close to this extraordinarily powerful object but also the government of Sri Lanka treats it as a national treasure. A fascinating, but unfortunate, consequence of this is that Tamil rebels have repeatedly tried to capture it for political gain (Tambiah 1992).

Cults of amulets, stupas, and other objects are not, as some might contend, a later corruption of true Buddhist practice. Recent archaeological interpretations by Schopen suggest that the worship of such sacred traces dates back to the time of the early Buddhist sangha. Epigraphical inscriptions in caves and other places where Buddhist clergy lived reveal that monks and nuns used to worship Buddhist books and other repositories of power that were associated in some way with the Buddha himself. They believed that such behavior could grant them eternal life or rebirth as a god (Schopen 1997). Thus, it seems that all Buddhists, including the clergy, are quite religious . . . just like people everywhere.

Nun Sense

A cognitive approach to Buddhism also allows us to explain one more problem documented by the contemporary study of Buddhism . . . the absence of officially ordained Theravada nuns. Today, Buddhist monks, modernist and traditional alike, have rejected pleas to ordain nuns into the sangha on technical grounds related to the *Vinaya-Pitaka*. According to *Vinaya* law, both a senior nun and a senior monk have to be present for an ordination of a nun to take place. According to tradition, the Buddha himself established this law. Unfortunately, at some point in history, the Theravada nun lineage died out, and so there are no longer any nuns available to perform ordinations (Bartholomeusz 1994; N. Falk 1989; Kabilsingh 1991). On these grounds, contemporary monks are refusing to ordain a new lineage of nuns. "The Buddha said so" is their stance.

There are, as you might imagine, critics of this stance. Aspiring nuns (called *mae jii*) in Thailand, for example, have all but ignored the ruling and proceeded to live like nuns regardless. Feminists, both in the West and in Asia, have spoken out against this policy, which they see as androcentric and patriarchal. And other scholars of Buddhism have even questioned the authority of the *Vinaya* itself. Yet most monks and lay Buddhists refuse to budge (Gross 1993; Kabilsingh 1991). Why?

The most popular reason cited by critics is that either (or both) the tradition of Buddhism itself or its current administrators are sexist (e.g., Bartholomeusz 1994; Gross 1993; Kabilsingh 1991). However, this will not do. This answer does not, in fact, explain much at all. It merely restates the question by shifting the problem (the widespread existence of sexism in Buddhist cultures becomes the new problem to be explained). A better explanation can be made by appeals to the cognitive constraints of ritual form.

Recall that the ritual form hypothesis of McCauley and Lawson (2002) explained why religious rituals come in two types. In special agent rituals, superhuman agents, via an ordained ritual officiate, do things to people (e.g., baptisms, or weddings), and in special patient rituals, people do things to superhuman agents (e.g., sacrificial offerings). Each type of ritual has, in turn, specific rules that guide the ritual's performance. Special agent rituals are only performed once because, since the agents of the ritual action are superhuman agents, their effects are "superpermanent." Special patient rituals, however, are repeatable. Moreover, special agent rituals are accompanied by "high-sensory pageantry," which makes the event meaningful and memorable (after all—it's an important event!). In contrast, special patient rituals are relatively unemotional, if not humdrum. Rituals that involve you doing the action to a superhuman agent are done often and without much fanfare, but special agent rituals in which gods do things to you are quite exciting.

One of the central special agent rituals of the Theravada ritual system is ordination into the sangha. The performance of an ordination is one of the most important events in the life of a Buddhist, and so these occasions are often celebrated community-wide, with highly festive activities such as singing, dancing, feasting, and gift giving. Furthermore, the rules for ordinations are ages old. They date all the way back to the Buddha, who is claimed to have performed the very first ordination ritual. McCauley and Lawson have termed such rituals (i.e., first performance rituals) "theoretical rituals" because such rituals only have to exist theoretically for members of the system to follow their rules. This means that whether or not the Buddha actually performed the very first special agent ritual is irrelevant; the rules are followed because Buddhists believe he did. In the case of Buddhism, the rules most certainly are followed.

The structures of ritual systems thus determine how rituals are to be performed. In general, special agent rituals follow from the rules established by the superhuman agent, who is often the founder of the religion (e.g., Christ, Buddha). As such, because superhuman agents start rituals, the buck stops with them as well. Any time questions arise about what can and cannot be done to change a ritual, leaders of religious groups tend to appeal to the guidelines, whether real or imagined, established long ago by the superhuman agent in the original theoretical ritual. No matter what conscious claims participants make about the nature of the founder of a religion, in terms of ritual structure, they serve as superhuman agents. The Buddha, by means of his authority in establishing the very first (theoretical) rituals, is a central superhuman agent.

This account helps explain contemporary Buddhists' rigid refusal to ordain nuns. Despite what modernists, reformers, and other "atheistic" Buddhist monks might say, when it comes to ordaining nuns—which would involve breaking the rules of the Vinaya—they simply won't disobey the guidelines of the law because the law was established by the Buddha. In this sense, the Buddha clearly, though tacitly, functions as a superhuman agent.

Keeping the Buddha in Mind

The preceding examples suggest how the understanding of Buddhism, and of religion by extension, might be clarified by knowing how human cognition works. If humans simply learned religion from their theological traditions, then we would find no gap between the "ought" and the "is" in Buddhism or any other religion. Yet Buddhism "on the ground" is significantly different from Buddhism "in the texts." Some of the differences are harmless, such as those that involve legendary folk tales about the impressive stature and superhuman abilities of the Buddha. Others, however, like the refusal to ordain women, are susceptible to criticism.

In addition, what's also important for our purposes is that Buddhism does not stand out as an anomaly in the comparative study of religion. The very same issues that affect other religions are

found in Buddhism. We find in Buddhism the widespread postu-
lation of superhuman agents, the performance of rituals that adhere
to cognitively constrained rules and guidelines and (for better or
worse) contestations and refutations of what follows from the system's traditions. The latter point is instructive. Buddhists are human beings and therefore employ economical reasoning strategies
for most cognitive tasks; therefore, Buddhist theology becomes
merely one type of knowledge that informs what people think and
do. Being human beings, Buddhists draw on more basic knowledge, such as tacit theories of the world constrained by intuitive
ontology, which they have acquired genetically and developmen-
tally. Thus, Buddhists are not passive recipients of Buddhism. They
are active participants in it. In this sense, they are like members of
every religion. And so Buddhism is the same as other religions because its members share the same cognitive equipment as members
of other religions. This means that Buddhism does not challenge
our ability to compare religions. For, as it turns out, all religions,
including Buddhism, have deeply structured recurring features.
They are all constrained by human cognition.

CHAPTER FIVE

W.D.G.D.? (WHAT DOES GOD DO?)

Since its original publication in 1981, Harold Kushner's book *When Bad Things Happen to Good People* has sold thousands of copies worldwide. Something about it struck a chord. The message of the book was supposed to be "inspirational" because it tried to convince its readers, primarily Jews and Christians, that the belief in God should not be threatened by the reality of evil and suffering in the world. In other words, fear not, because despite the way it looks sometimes, there is a God. The evil and suffering we see in the world is our own doing, and that is good news: if we cause it, we can stop it.

Kushner's book engaged a problem that has preoccupied theologians for centuries, namely the problem of "theodicy." From the Greek *theos* (god) and *dike* (justice), theodicy is the problem of explaining "God's justice" in the world. In short, it is the problem of explaining why, if there is a God, evil and innocent suffering exist. The theological problem can be formulated as follows:

1. God exists.
2. God created the world.
3. God is entirely good.
4. God is entirely powerful.

Yet:

5. Evil and innocent suffering exist.

Obviously, this is a problem because:

6. If God can't prevent evil, then God must not be entirely powerful.

Or:

7. If God won't prevent evil, then God must not be entirely good.

Therefore:

8. If God exists, he can't be entirely good or entirely powerful.

Because:

9. Evil and innocent suffering exist.

This problem has preoccupied theologians and philosophers for centuries, and they have generated sophisticated, though arguably unsatisfactory (Hume 1977; Pojman 2001, pp. 67–80) solutions to it (Augustine 1955; Hick 1966; Plantinga 1990). However, this problem is not just a dilemma for intellectuals. It is a problem for most religious people because it concerns the heart of what religion is all about: agency.

The distinctive feature of religion is the presumption that superhuman agents exist. The use of the term "agent" here is critical because what drives religions is the presumption that superhuman agents have the power to *control* events in the world. By some theological accounts, deities have total control (e.g., Calvin 1936). Were they not to have this power, as the problem of theodicy suggests, the gods would not merit much reverence.

Or are deities in control? I have noted that research suggests that religious believers don't necessarily think that gods are in control of most of the events in the world. Recall from chapter 3 that, when asked, Christians will say, to be "theologically correct," that God knows and controls all. Yet when they are asked questions that require them to make inferences about divine agency, researchers find that they view God as a much more limited agent than their ascribed theology suggests. Despite what theological ideas they've learned—and "believe"—people still think they have an "internal locus of control" (J. L. Barrett 1999; Barrett & Keil 1996; Barrett & Nyhof 2001; Lupfer, Brock, & DePaola 1992; Lupfer, DePaola, Brock, & Clement 1994; Lupfer, Tolliver, &

Jackson 1996; Spilka & Schmidt, 1983; Spilka, Shaver, & Kirkpatrick 1985). Despite their religious beliefs, people nonetheless believe that human beings or other mundane agents (mechanical processes, other people, etc.) are the causes of most of life's events (Sperber, Premack, & Premack 1995). Thus, there is a tension in religion between theological determinism (events are controlled by God) and free will (events are controlled by human beings). This tension results from the ambiguity of agency.

Mental Tricks

I hope it is clear by now that religious people don't behave the way sociologists and anthropologists have long thought. People don't simply learn what to think by learning theology. If that were the case, there would be no variation within religions at all because everyone would think the same thoughts (i.e., the official theology) and new religious ideas would never be generated. For one to come to believe a religious idea, one would have to learn it. To learn it, one would have to hear it from someone else. For someone else to know it, that person would have to have learned it from someone else, and on and on and on. Yet we know that new religious ideas emerge all the time. Therefore, if it is possible for people to have original ideas at all, then learning must not be entirely passive. And, given the variety of ideas that float around in any given culture, we must conclude that people actively generate ideas. Thus, we are back to square one . . . what effect does religion actually have on people?

Obviously, much of religious thought involves attributions about why things happen. Religion, as many have noted, explains stuff. As Bernard Spilka and his colleagues have noted,

> Scriptures and theologies have told how the universe was created, why humans occupy a special place in the scheme of things, why seasonal changes and natural disasters occur, why some people triumph while others fail, and why everyone must occasionally suffer and eventually die. (1985, p. 1)

Geertz has argued similarly that religion constructs for people a "worldview" and an "ethos," which provide people with a view of and for the world (Geertz 1973). Religious ideas, according to this view, provide explanations of the world and its workings that, once learned, instruct people in how to think and act. Religious people, then, ought to believe what their religious traditions teach them—they ought to think superhuman agents are the causes of all world events. Yet we know that this is not the case. In fact, it seems to be rarely the case.

Try this. Stand up and look down at your feet. Now lift one foot in the air and stand on the other for two seconds. Now sit back down.

What caused you to do this? Did God? Or did you do this by your own free will? Most likely, your instinctual answer is that you did it on your own. On reflection you might postulate that it was all a part of "God's plan." If so, your cognitive efforts would be in line with how many religious people think. Your instinctive, or "online," answer is that you did it. Yet, if you believe that God is in control, then you might, on "offline" reflection, change your mind: God made me do it.

Online thinking involves making rapid judgments about things without much reflective thought. Offline thinking is more slowed-down and reflective. As such, offline thinking allows individuals to draw on learned schema, including supernatural schema, to fulfill cognitive tasks. Your online answer to what caused you to get up, look at your feet, stand on one foot, and then sit down was most likely "in order to participate in your little game, I stood up and looked down at my feet." On reflection, however, were you a religious person you might invoke a different schema altogether . . . maybe God (or the Devil) made you do it.

In this sense online thinking involves the employment of non-cultural, probably naturalistic, schemas. No one had to teach you that if you want to stand up you have to make a choice to do it and then act on that choice. You intuitively know that you have "self-agency."

Yet, depending on how well you know the established theology of your religion, you might invoke a "theologically correct" idea in your schematic account. You might have learned at some point the doctrinal notion that God controls everything. Using this supernatural schema you might deduce that God controls your actions: if (1) God controls everything, and (2) you perform an action, then (3) God must have caused you to perform an action. This is theologically correct, but few people actually think like this online. Thus one of the most important tasks for psychologists is to explain how, when, and in what contexts people attribute events to religious causes.

Intuitive Metaphysics

As discussed in chapter 3, attribution is a central feature of human cognition. We are able to represent in our minds what's happening in the world around us. We are able to infer causes and to make predictions about how things will happen in the future. Consider the cognition of infants and toddlers. Normal, healthy babies know from very early on that moms and dads cause lots of things to happen. Moms and dads (ideally) supply food, change messy diapers, give hugs, and so forth. Eventually, babies learn that they can cause things to happen, like cause moms and dads to give them food or change their messy diapers. One of the best strategies for accomplishing these goals is to cry . . . loudly.

Much of human cognition involves trying to make sense of the world by differentiating what sorts of things are in the world, how those things work, and how we can (or can't) control them. The central features of the world then tend to be agents, because not only do agents cause many of the most important events in our world but also we can influence them (for benefits). Thus, much of our cognitive development involves honing our understanding of agency and therefore of causality.

According to most cognitive scientists, human beings represent four domain-specific types of causality in the world: physical, biological, psychological, and social (Sperber et al. 1995). When a rock smashes through a glass window, the cause of the shattering is physical—the force of the rock's momentum and the hardness of the rock's mass exceeded the strength of the glass to withstand the physical force of the moving rock. Explaining the scientific physics of an event like this is complicated, but human beings nevertheless understand it quite well instinctively. We don't have to learn that hard things crash into each other.

In addition to physical causality, humans also naturally represent biological causality. We know that biological things (plants, animals, and people) are born, grow, eat, drink, and die. Moreover, humans recognize that certain types of objects have psychological (and social, when in groups) agency. Psychological agency is predicated on the capacity for "self-propelledness." While rocks must be launched to move, agents move by their own volition. If your dog wants a treat, it walks up to you and begs. Agents can do this, our cognitive equipment informs us, because they have minds.

Human beings spend a great deal of time engaging the domain of psychological causality because much of our survival depends on how well we interact with the agents around us. It is logical then to understand how a hyperactive agency detection device might be adaptive. Agents cause most events, and so having a brain that is primed to detect agency is a wonderful tool for survival. Consider the event in which a person flips a switch on the wall and the lights of a room come on. Consider when someone punches another person in the face, and the next day that person has a bruised eye. Consider when a person throws a ball over the backyard fence and into a creek. Few people would have trouble inferring the cause of these events: people.

Though effective, our causal cognition is not perfect. Consider the ambiguities in certain types of court cases. Should McDonald's be held responsible for burns from a spilled cup of coffee? Should a woman who kills her spouse be held responsible, if she is overcome by rage after years of abuse? What if a woman who is "hormonally imbalanced" due to her menstrual cycle kills? Should she be held responsible, or couldn't she stop herself? What about mentally handicapped individuals or persons with schizophrenia? Are they truly responsible for their actions?

The lesson in these ambiguous cases, as all first-year law students learn, is that the causes of events are not always clear. Yet we, including judges and juries, often need/want to find someone at fault for events. The intuitive need to find a cause (in these cases, a "fault") for events underlies most intuitive theories of justice: responsible parties must be punished. Our intuitive inclination to identify causes is very strong, and that inclination drives judgments even in cases where causes are ambiguous.

Religion exploits this basic human capacity. Given our predisposition to seek causes, we abductively invoke agents. Thus it is no coincidence that the central features of religion are superhuman agents. Recall the paradigmatic theories in the cognitive science of religion. Guthrie has argued that religion is a form of anthropomorphism (Guthrie 1993). Boyer has shown that representations of supernatural agents violate default expectations about natural agents

(Boyer 1994, 2001). Lawson and McCauley have shown that ritual structures are constrained by a built-in "action-representation-system" that is itself dependent on the cognitive capacity to identify agents performing actions in the world (Lawson & McCauley 1990; McCauley & Lawson 2002). And of course Justin Barrett and his colleagues have shown that religious believers tend to "naturalize" supernatural agents; that is, when making online judgments, we represent superhuman agents as having very humanlike capacities (J. L. Barrett 1999, 2001; Barrett & Keil 1996; Barrett & Nyhof 2001).

Thus, some psychologists have begun to conclude that religious ideas are representations that postulate hidden causes of events. This seems to be especially common when the causes of events are ambiguous, a phenomenon known as the "God in the gaps" hypothesis (Lupfer et al. 1996). According to this view, humans infer superhuman agents as causes whenever "regular" causes cannot be identified, and experimental research seems to confirm this hypothesis.

If theology doesn't determine people's worldviews, then what are we to think about religion at all? Again, though religion doesn't determine people's worldviews, it does not follow from this principle that religion doesn't influence people's worldviews at all. Rather, human beings are more likely to believe and employ a religious idea if it is (fairly) consistent with the accords of everyday cognitive concepts and inferences. While almost any theology can be memorized, those with the most "inferential potential" are going to be invoked for cognitive tasks (Boyer 1994, 2001).

Inferential Potential and Cultural Ideas

As noted in chapter 3, Boyer's view is that religious ideas are most likely to be transmittable if they achieve a cognitive optimum. Ideas that achieve a cognitive optimum are those that are nonnatural but learnable (Boyer 1994, 2001). This theory is based on research in cognitive psychology about what sorts of ideas come naturally to human minds. Natural in this sense means innate only insofar as the various kinds of tacit default assumptions in our intuitive ontology are not learned from culture. Rather, an intuitive ontology, and its related capacities, is required to learn cultural ideas. Humans know tacitly, again, that natural objects, artifacts, plants, animals, and humans populate the world. Furthermore, humans know that nonliving objects cannot move on their own, but living things (plants, animals, humans) can. And we know that psychological agents have minds.

Some ideas that humans have, however, are acquired. For example, children in the United States, the United Kingdom, Australia, and other English-speaking countries learn that big, gray, peanut-eating animals with long trunks and tails are "elephants." In Thailand, children learn that these animals are "chaang."

Furthermore, children learn ideas that are counterintuitive. For example, school children learn in science classes that the sun does not move around the Earth, despite the fact that we see it do just that every single day of our lives. In this sense, many people spend their adult lives holding quite contradictory ideas simultaneously: that the sun is stationary yet rises in the east and sets in the west each day and night. According to Boyer, religious ideas function in the same way. Because they are nonnatural and counterintuitive, religious ideas provide one conceptual scheme among others.

Consider the properties of a religious agent. In Christianity, God is postulated as a grand being who has perfect knowledge and vision, doesn't need food or water to survive, and is physically and biologically immortal (in this sense He's quite like the Buddha). Notice that each of these traits violates our intuitive expectations about what agents are like. Natural agents have certain physical, biological, and psychological properties: they are limited in space, don't have perfect knowledge or perfect vision (which is why we can trick them!), need food and water to live, and will eventually die (at least a biological death). God concepts violate those intuitive expectations.

The naturalness of employing counterintuitive concepts makes better sense when we consider science. Recall the case of the setting sun. Nearly all Americans know that the sun doesn't move around the Earth, and yet nearly all treat it as if it does. Only in situations that require the recall of learned ideas about planetary motion will most people invoke their astronomical wisdom (assuming they paid attention in science class). Likewise, religious people do not necessarily alter their way of viewing the world once they've internalized a given theology. In some contexts they will invoke such thoughts. In others they won't.

The constraints of cognition impose selective pressures on religious concepts. Generally speaking, naturalistic ideas will be invoked for most cognitive tasks (e.g., the flip of the switch caused the lights to come on, throwing the ball through a window caused the window to break, punching me in the nose caused my black eye, etc.). However, in some contexts, supernatural ideas might be employed. Yet, among religious ideas, those that are minimally counterintuitive are more likely to be employed for online problem solving. This means, therefore, that over time, those religious ideas with the most inferential potential are more likely to survive than others.

The history of mainline Christianity in the United States provides an excellent case study for testing this hypothesis. Since the United States is a relatively young country, it is flush with material documents that provide historians with enough data to reconstruct the basic patterns of religiosity of Americans. Some of the earliest "settlers," the Puritans, tried but failed to enforce a maximally counterintuitive theological tradition (Calvinism). What historians of American religious history tell us confirms the hypothesis: given the selective pressures on religious concepts, mainline American religious beliefs should over time settle at a node of minimal counterintuitiveness. This is precisely what has happened. Most Americans are Arminianists (Arminianism means belief in free will [i.e., self-agency] and in divine sovereignty) even though one of the most dominant forms of Christian theology at the founding of this country was Calvinism (Calvinism means belief in absolute divine sovereignty). The rise to dominance of Arminianism in U.S. religion is an instructive example not only of how human cognition constrains cultural possibilities but also of how a deep grasp of cognition can help scholars make sense of why historical movements occur as they do. I will now explore this development.

Protestant Christianity in Colonial America

Various tribal nations now known as the Native Americans populated North America for thousands of years before the arrival of the Europeans in the late fifteenth and early sixteenth centuries. However, the arrival of the Europeans and their various forms of Christianity marked the beginnings of what would become mainline American religion (Ahlstrohm 1972; Marty 1984; Williams 2001). Among the many Christian groups to settle the New World, the Puritans had arguably the most profound effect. The Puritans were officially members of the Church of England, but they had been deeply influenced by the theology of Calvin while living on the European continent during the reign of Queen Mary (1553–58). A small number of "separating" Puritans, fed up with the status quo in England, left for the North American colonies as "pilgrims," seeking to build a "New Jerusalem" where religious and moral purity would reign.

They were known as the Puritans for their rigid adherence to a "pure" version of Christianity. The Calvinism they had adopted was a deterministic theology based on the logical conclusion of the doctrine of divine sovereignty. If, the logic went, God is the creator of the world, is active in the world, is all-knowing, and is all-powerful, the fate of the world must be already determined according to His will and plan. Therefore, the salvation of each human being, as well as the fate of Christian societies, has already been worked out in advance by God Himself. To say the least, Puritan theology preached a radical "external locus of control."

The separating Puritans who settled the area near Plymouth Rock and later merged with the larger Massachusetts Bay Colony were instrumental in establishing the "Protestant work ethic" that over time would spread throughout the colonies (Weber 1976). Central to the "New England way" of religion was the church. Puritan communities became famous for their lengthy church services marked by fiery sermons (some lasting all day) meticulously prepared by trained clergy. In addition, sociopolitical decisions, not to mention legal judgments, were made in accordance with the dictates of Puritan doctrine. The operative assumption in Puritan society was the awesome power of God.

Yet, if cognitive theories of religion are correct, the maximally counterintuitive doctrines of orthodox Calvinism should have little staying power. Believing that God controls everything precludes human agency and therefore should have little online inferential potential. In other words, because Calvinism removes agency entirely from the human world, it would most likely not be invoked in online thinking. When humans are required to infer causes, they resort to default (i.e., natural) inferences about psychological agency and so Puritan doctrine should have little chance of successful transmission over the long run. Is this the case?

Evidence confirms this prediction on two accounts. First, historians of colonial America have discovered that despite their efforts at theological correctness, the Puritans were not strict theological determinists. The Puritans were instead much more "Jeremidian" than Calvinist: like the biblical prophet Jeremiah, they interpreted the hands of superhuman agency at work in all events of misfortune and suffering, but their interpretations seemed to suggest that humans were being punished for misdeeds of their own doing (Stulman 1998). Thus strict laws were enacted as a deterrent to immoral behavior—as if humans could control themselves.

Moreover, Puritans also followed the *Farmer's Almanac*, astrology, and other means of divining events, and they greatly feared anything that seemed to reveal the workings of witches and other demonic agents (few events of American religious history are as infamous as the witch trials in Salem, Massachusetts, in the seventeenth century). And in further display of theological incorrectness, Puritan society was replete with rituals and other activities, like fasts, confessions, and natural healings that were felt to be able to engender favorable outcomes in this world (Hall 1989; Karlsen 1989; Stout 1986).

In addition to the popular dimensions of Puritan religion, a second bit of evidence confirming the instability of determinism thesis is the demise of Calvinism during the "Great Awakenings" of the eighteenth century. The Great Awakenings were short-lived (five to ten years) but powerful periods in U.S. religious history when emotionally charged "revivals" of religion swept through the colonial countryside, bringing to people the kind of Protestant Christianity we now recognize as "evangelicalism" (Bushman 1970; Butler 1990; McLoughlin 1978; Ward 1992). The first Great Awakening (1730s–1740s) was a loose conglomerate of street-corner gatherings, open church services, tent revivals, camp meetings, and so forth, during which charismatic preachers like Jonathan Edwards, James Davenport, and George Whitefield brought scores of men and women to highly emotional conversion experiences called "First Blessings." Receiving a First Blessing entailed not just passively understanding the preacher's message but openly repenting for sins and asking for the Lord's forgiveness right there on the spot. These conversion experiences were so significant that those who "got religion" were said to have been "born again."

The catalyst for these experiences was the fiery extemporaneous sermons delivered by preacher-men who felt "called by the Spirit of God" to spread the word of the Bible. Their dramatic orations were supplemented with arousing activities like hymn-singing, spectacular personal testimonials, and in some cases full-immersion adult baptisms . . . all of which had as the primary goal generating emotionally charged religious experiences among the audience (Bushman 1970; Butler 1990; Ward 1992). However, sermons were the featured event, and the sermons were meant specifically to cultivate a "religion of the heart." Interestingly, to reach the hearts of men and women, they often had to stray from the theological traditions of orthodox Calvinism (i.e., "religion of the head"). The message shifted from the Puritan-Calvinists' emphasis on the awesome power of God to the Arminianist emphasis on the role of self-agency: salvation was not predetermined; one had to *achieve* it by reaching out to God. Consciously or not, the Great Awakenings brought Arminianism to the masses.

Why was Arminianism more appealing than Calvinism? Though most sociohistorical analyses of colonial Christianity focus on the environmental conditions surrounding the Great Awakenings (e.g., Calvinism vs. Arminianism corresponds with elite vs. popular, urban vs. rural, industrial vs. agricultural, New England vs. Midwest, etc.), I believe that the selective pressures imposed on conceptual transmission by the limited processing constraints of cognition best account for this historical development. In contrast to the rigid predestination of Calvinism, Arminianists preached a "cooperative theology" in which salvation was achieved by the dual efforts of God and humans. An often-used Arminanist image was that humans needed to reach up and grab God's outreached hand to be saved. Thus the Arminianist conceptual scheme allowed for the invocation of self-agency (i.e., free will). If you think of this development as a competition for survival, Arminianism won because it was better suited for successful transmission.

Cognition and Free Will

How do cognitive theories illuminate this series of events? First, Guthrie's theory offers the beginnings of an explanation for why the Puritans were awestruck by the power of superhuman agents that they believed surrounded them. As noted earlier, the Puritans were Jeremidian insofar as they believed that misfortunes were proof that humans were, in the famous words of Jonathan Edwards, "sinners in the hands of an angry God" (Edwards 1957). Boyer's theory extends Guthrie's point by showing why such an idea would have been attractive to the Puritans in the first place: namely, such an idea represents God as an agent with perfect knowledge and awesome power (though materially invisible).

Most important, however, Barrett's theory of theological correctness instructs us to distinguish the online popular ideas and actions of the Puritans from the offline theological ideas, and to keep in mind that the humans are capable of holding both. The capacity for holding multiple levels of representation explains why, if the Calvinistic Puritans "believed in" divine sovereignty, they also "believed in" witchcraft, astrology, religious conversion, and the causal relationship between self-effort and worldly success.

The online/offline distinction further shows that minimally counterintuitive religious representations, that is, those that are close to naturalistic representations, will have a greater likelihood of transmission than maximally counterintuitive representations. Minimally counterintuitive ideas are easy to learn, and, more important, they are easier to recall than maximally counterintuitive ideas, which are cognitively burdensome. In the case in question, Calvinism proves to be less likely to survive over the long run because it is a burdensome idea that precludes the role of human agency. Arminianism, in contrast, maintains the same inferential potential about superhuman agency as Calvinism—Arminianists also believe that God has divine sovereignty—but supplements it with human agency.

Given the rich inferential potential of Arminianism, we should not be surprised that in situations where such ideas are preached, they would be enthusiastically received. The revival meetings of the Great Awakenings seem to confirm this. Not only did revival meetings attract scores of interested folks, the participants often plunged into ecstatic neuromuscular "exercises" that included laughing, dancing, falling down, jerking, and even barking like rabid dogs (Brown 1992; Sims 1996).

Conceptual Tacking

But what do people do once they "get" religion? It's uncontroversial that religious ideas inform religious actions, but how so is an important question I'd like to answer. Cognitive scientists of religion are clear on one point: religious representations are triggered in human mind-brains. The question at stake, however, is do religious ideas motivate religious behavior?

The sermons, songs, and shouts of the Awakening revivals clearly motivated certain types of religious experiences. The environments of revival meetings were occasions of what McCauley and Lawson and Whitehouse call "high-sensory pageantry" (Lawson & McCauley 1990; McCauley & Lawson 2002; Whitehouse 1995, 2000). According to these scholars, high-sensory pageantry in ritual performance aids memory, salience, and transmission of representations by evoking strong emotional responses. Such experiences are commonly induced through physical stimulae like singing, dancing, shouting, sleep deprivation, and numerous other arousing behaviors. In addition, the efficacy of preaching during the Great Awakenings (not to mention today—consider the powerful role preaching plays in evangelical denominations like Holiness-Pentecostal churches) suggests that intense emotional responses are enhanced by engagement with attention-grabbing conceptual schemes. Physiological changes that underwrite extraordinary experiences can be stimulated verbally (e.g., intimidation, manipulation, flattery, reinforcement), especially when the ideas being communicated have rich inferential potential. The Great Awakenings reveal a recipe for successful transmission of religious ideas.

What follows from this account of the revivals is that effective preaching exploits the basic processes of human cognition. Given that much of human reasoning involves making inductive runs through multiple schema in search of the "best" (given the circumstances) representation for a given situation, preaching that is similar to this style of thought is likely to be effective. Examination of preaching styles during the Awakenings reveals that preachers engaged in precisely this kind of thinking. One of the most effective preaching strategies was what I will call, to borrow a metaphor from sailing, conceptual "tacking." In sailing, whenever a captain seeks to sail into the wind, the boat is maneuvered back and forth strategically at approximately forty-five-degree angles to take advantage of the wind's direction and power. Preachers employ a similar strategy by shifting back and forth, providing explanations of ordinary events in terms of supernatural causes. Revivalist preachers engaged their audience in a complex cognitive dialectic that involved (1) diagnostic reasoning, in which general causes are inferred "backward" from particular events, and (2) causal reasoning, in which future events are inferred probabilistically from the represented characteristics of the postulated causative agent (Kahneman, Slovic, & Tversky 1982).

Religious conceptual tacking involves not only explaining mundane events in terms of supernatural causes (i.e., superhuman agents) but also making inferences about potential events from what is presumed about the causer. This is a powerful recipe for belief. Misfortunes are caused by the devil. Illnesses result from being possessed. Financial windfalls are a gift from God. If you don't obey divine mandates, your future will be dire. Such abductive reasoning exploits natural styles of thought. This strategy, combined with the salience of religious representations, is very effective.

Ritual Predictions

The final dimension of a robust cognitive account of the dynamics of early American Protestantism should involve considerations of the psychological constraints on ritual actions, such as those described by the ritual form hypothesis (Lawson & McCauley 1990; McCauley & Lawson 2002). According to this theory, the actions performed in any given ritual system conform to cognitive constraints about representations of action. Thus, religious systems must balance the special agent rituals (those rituals in which humans are recipients of actions from the gods via priests) and special patient rituals (those in which gods are the recipients of actions from humans). This theory allows for the prediction that if a religious ritual system becomes unbalanced, that is, has too much of one type and too little of the other, then significant changes related to the structural form of those rituals will result. This seems also to have happened in early American Protestantism.

The central rituals of Protestantism are usually communion and baptism. In Puritan communities, however, the latter took on an additional role as "civic regulator." Puritan theology held a doctrine of "limited atonement" of the "visible saints." This meant that only those limited few whom God had preelected were enabled salvation by Jesus' sacrificial crucifixion, and that the (pre)elected would show their elect status by living morally upright lives. Their saintliness would be visible behaviorally. Thus, according to the dictates of the doctrine of limited atonement, only the elect were fit to be baptized (after all, what would be the use in baptizing others?). However, the nonelect were also required to attend church, obey the laws, and participate in social activities for the purposes of engendering the Kingdom of God on Earth (which required keeping the Devil in check). As it turned out, only about one in five New Englanders were considered to be members of the elect (Williams 2001).

The principle of baptizing only the elect, and thus providing full membership/citizenship, became a problem in the successive generations of Puritan families whose children and grandchildren didn't follow the predicted pattern of experiencing a conversion event. To address this, the Puritan leaders created what became known as the "Half-Way Covenant," which allowed individuals with ambiguous statuses to be baptized "half-way" in hopes that some day they would come to realize, fully, their elect status. As a result of this decision, baptism lost its importance in the church. Its role in the church was "deflated," to use the language of McCauley and Lawson (2002), and became less important than the taking of the Eucharist in the performance of communion. As McCauley and Lawson's theory would predict, during the Great Awakenings many Puritans (now called Congregationalist) and Presbyterians converted to the Baptist denomination, whose central feature was "believer-baptism," a special agent ritual with high-sensory pageantry and correspondingly high levels of emotionality (McLoughlin 1971; Payne 1998).

The Big Picture

Rituals and other religious activities, as noted earlier, seem to follow from religious concepts. Yet the religious concepts do not determine, per se, what follows. Rather, it appears that cognitive processes drive the thoughts and actions of religious believers at both the individual and the cultural levels. In the case of early American Protestantism, the Calvinism of the Puritans was short-lived because Calvinist theology was too cognitively burdensome to be employed online or to be maintained over the long run. Thus it is not surprising that the Puritans were prone, according to orthodox Calvinism, to theological incorrectness. Nor should we be surprised that Arminianism came to dominate mainline American Protestant thought.

The latter point is illuminating because it suggests that religious ideas with maximum inferential potential can even spread across diverse populations, such as in the United States. Ideas like "co-operative theology" (i.e., Arminianism; belief in both divine sovereignty and free will) are very attractive to human beings across the board because they exploit natural cognitive processes. Theism in general necessarily contains an internal conceptual tension between the powers of the gods and the powers of people. Therefore, though awkward, religious conceptual schemes that alleviate that tension successfully will be selected over those that don't.

Arminianism still dominates American Protestant thought today. There are at present only a few remaining orthodox Calvinists in the United States, and even they seem to possess an internal locus of control (J. L. Barrett 1999). Moreover, conservative evangelicals today preach that God has absolute sovereignty yet blame humanity for the world's problems. Recently, after the attacks of September 11, 2001, Jerry Falwell argued—in a very Jeremidian manner—that the attacks were a result of the moral lapse of American society. His "evidence" was the widespread existence of "sins" like homosexuality, feminism, and the American Civil Liberties Union.

The conceptual tension between divine sovereignty and free will, which has preoccupied some of the greatest minds in history, is a natural tension in Christianity that results from how the mind works. Since humans rely so heavily on notions of self-/human agency, it is difficult to believe that superhuman agents control everything. Yet, if they don't, what exactly is the nature of their power?

Yet, to be fair, this conceptual tension is not unique to American Protestant Christianity. Since religious reasoning is constrained by human cognition, and human cognition is essentially the same across cultures, we can predict with confidence that this tension recurs across cultures. Preliminary ethnographic and experimental evidence confirms this (Barrett & Keil 1996; Boyer 2001). Regardless of tradition, great minds in all religions have wrestled with the ambiguity of agency. Buddhists disagree on whether they can achieve nirvana on their own or need the help of a Buddha or bodhisattva. Muslims simultaneously say that Allah wills everything that happens in the world yet struggle to bring about his divine will, however imagined (e.g., *jihad*). And Christians, like Jews, Wiccans, Rastafarians, and religious people everywhere labor to decipher how best to live life—a struggle that results in the oscillation between "doing" God's will and "giving in" to it. Such is the way of religious reasoning.

CHAPTER SIX

I'D RATHER BE LUCKY THAN GOOD

Armando Benitez has been betting on horses for over forty years. According to his own testimony, he has tried every trick in the book to win. The best chances for winning, however, seem to contradict everything you might assume about how to bet. Instead of using "scientific" methods, like basing bets on a horse's past performances, insider knowledge, track conditions, and so on, he takes a novice to the track and asks that person to pick a horse for him. In a surprisingly high number of cases, the novice picks correctly. What is the explanation? "Beginner's luck" seems to work at the track (Bechtel & Stains 1997).

Setting aside momentarily the question of whether or not the novice's picks really are lucky, what is interesting about the story is that it doesn't sound completely absurd. I would be willing to bet (pun intended) that nearly every person has experienced some unlikely event that can only be explained as resulting from luck. How else can we explain individuals who win the lottery or win thousands of dollars on a slot machine in a casino, or randomly find a hundred-dollar bill in the street? How can we explain the fortune of those people who stayed home from work in the World Trade Center on September 11, 2001, or those who for some reason or another missed their scheduled flights on the hijacked planes that same morning? How can we explain even minor incidents like getting caught in traffic while late for an important meeting, or having your computer crash just before your project is due? All of these events, whatever the "ultimate" or "real" cause, are attributable to luck.

Luck beliefs come to us quite easily. Consider the plethora of superstitions in the West. It is good luck to find your initials in a spider web. If the numbers of your birth date add up to a number that can be divided by seven, you'll be lucky all of your life. Telling entertainers to "break a leg" sends them good luck. Shooting stars are a sign of good luck. You'll be lucky if you accidentally wear clothing on the wrong side out all day long; if a strange dog follows you; if a swallow builds a nest on your house; if a frog enters your home; if you see three butterflies together; or if you throw salt over your shoulder. In contrast, it is bad luck to tell an entertainer "Good luck!" The number thirteen is unlucky, which is why many hotels have no thirteenth floor. It is bad luck to walk under a ladder; to cross the path of a black cat; to not wear your lucky charm or to not perform the usual ritual in preparation for a big game (Bechtel & Stains 1997; Radford & Radford 1969; Seligman 1968; Shermer 1997; Singer & Singer 1995; Vyse 1997).

The list of "luck beliefs" is extensive. Bechtel and Stains's (1997) book about good luck is 374 pages long and averages about one luck belief per page. Radford and Radford's *Encyclopedia of Superstitions* (1969) is 264 pages long. What's more, both books are based mostly on luck beliefs found in Western cultures and so don't include the many luck beliefs circulating in the rest of the world, even though the belief in luck is not a "Western" invention, as some cultural relativists might assert.

Nor are luck beliefs only a "modern" (or only a premodern, if you prefer) phenomenon. There are examples of the belief in luck throughout history. In the first century C.E., Ovid is said to have proclaimed, "Luck affects everything. Let your hook always be cast in the stream. When you least expect it, there will be fish." The Christian patriarch Saint Augustine said, "The force of chance is diffused throughout the whole order of things." In Japan, *daruma* dolls, which are stylized replicas of a sixth-century Buddhist monk, are widely possessed as good-luck charms. Chinese calendars are created around "lucky" and "unlucky" times, as is the zodiac. In ancient Egypt, the hieroglyphic sign for the word "nefer" was used to represent goodness, beauty, happiness, youth, and good luck (Bechtel & Stains 1997).

Furthermore, people not only believe in luck but also perform rituals they believe (or hope) will improve their luck. And the list of luck rituals is also extensive. Throughout Asia, Buddhists purchase amulets to wear around their necks or hang in their cars, homes, and businesses in the hope of avoiding bad luck and attracting good luck (Earhart 1993, Southwold 1984; Spiro 1970; Swearer 1995; Tambiah 1984). In the Western world, people do the same. Catholic lay disciples of Saint Jude in the United States wear amulets to protect them from misfortune and to help them deal with "hopeless" causes (Orsi 1996). In Africa, both the Zulu and the Yoruba have religious specialists who strive, through ritual efforts, to ward off misfortune and mishap for the group (Lawson 1984). In the United States (and probably elsewhere) professional athletes perform a host of seemingly arbitrary actions designed to bring about good luck. Michael Jordan wore his college basketball shorts under his professional uniform. Hank Aaron wore the same shower shoes for his entire career. Jimmy Connors tucked a note from his grandmother in his socks during matches. Wade Boggs ate chicken before every baseball game he played, as did Jackie Joyner-Kersee before track meets (Bechtel & Stains 1997; Vyse 1997).

Again, the list of luck beliefs and practices is seemingly endless. Any cursory glance around the world reveals the widespread existence of such beliefs. Yet, despite this fact, little scholarly attention has been paid to it. For some reason, few people investigate this phenomenon, and most dismiss it as little more than superstition. However, the widespread belief in luck demands our attention not just because it is ubiquitous but because it reveals the complex workings of the mind. It should be uncontroversial by now that people must use the brains they have got to think and act, including thinking and acting religiously, and the brains they have work in specific ways. Given the ubiquitous belief in luck, it is safe to say that one way our brains operate is to reason abductively, especially about causality, since believing in luck involves abductive inferences about the "causes" (however ambiguous) of unlikely but personally important events. The belief in luck differs from religious belief only by degree because both involve the presumption of agency at work in the world. The essential difference is that the agents of religious traditions are less ambiguously represented than the "agents" of luck (although in some cases luck gets personified; e.g., "lukshmi" in Hinduism, "fortuna" in the ancient Near East, "lady luck" in Las Vegas, etc.).

Analyzing Luck

The concept of luck is actually quite complex and thus should not be dismissed as simply superstition or sloppy thinking. In a basic sense, luck is synonymous with chance. When individuals presume the workings of luck in their lives, though, they often "spin" the effects of luck to be positive or negative, as in having good luck or bad luck. Furthermore, although the presumption of luck (or chance) implies that events are beyond human control, much of the preoccupation with luck involves performing actions that are hoped to influence (namely improve) luck. Now, mix in this variable: that luck completely contradicts the theologies of Christianity and Buddhism (and most likely of all religions, though I'll limit this study to these two traditions). Obviously, something quite strange is going on.

Theologies are constructed deductively. Theologians begin with the foundational premises of faith, such as *God exists, God is good, God is powerful*, and so on, and then deduce from those premises conclusions to questions that concern them. According to the conventional view of religion, not to mention the view assumed by the sociocultural scholars of religion discussed in chapter 2, the followers of a religion supposedly learn the theological doctrines of a religious system, and then, once learned, the theology determines how one thinks (or ought to think). However, the widespread belief in luck challenges this hypothesis.

Since religion involves interacting with postulated (or presumed) agents, and agents control the events of the world, everything, it would seem deductively, is controlled. Hence, as we commonly hear people say, everything happens "for a reason." Luck should be what philosophers call a *non sequitur*. Luck beliefs should not follow from accepted theological beliefs, regardless of tradition. As I showed in chapter 5, this is not the case. We should not be surprised, therefore, given what we know about the ambiguity of agency, that individuals in South Asia and in America don't necessarily ascribe complete control to the postulated agents of Buddhism and Christianity. A consideration of some of the complexities of Buddhist and Christian theology help to understand why not.

Theology

Buddhist theology, like Christian theology, is quite complex. (Fortunately I can limit my attention to Buddhist views about causality, since luck beliefs turn on causal reasoning.) The central feature of Buddhist theology regarding causality is the doctrine of karma, the law of "action and the appropriate result of action." It is a basic law of cause and effect that regulates the workings of the world, that is, one reaps what one sows (Humphreys 1984). Thus there is no official problem of theodicy in Buddhism because there is no official "innocent" suffering—events are the result of human actions.

In Buddhist terms, any event that a person experiences is the consequence of previous action(s). If a person has good luck, it is because they have accumulated "merit" (Sanskrit: *punya karma*) by living a good (i.e., Buddhist) life. In contrast, those people who have bad luck are believed to be reaping the effects of *papa karma*, or demerit. This notion is captured by the popular Thai Buddhist saying *Thaam dii, dai dii; thaam chua, dai chua* ("Do good, get good; do evil, get evil").

It takes little cognitive effort to grasp the Buddhist conception of karma. It's a version of the "Golden Rule" that recurs across cultures (Ridley 1997). However, on reflection, Buddhist theology is much more complicated. Consider the fact that because humans live in groups, each individual's actions have effects on other people. This creates a complex "web" of karmic interaction in which the actions of each person affect, potentially, many different people. So who causes what? How do we locate, in Buddhist terms, the agent that caused the event, if all agents' actions are collectively interconnected? Furthermore, what about the complex notion that actions follow from a person's intentions, while a person's intentions result from previous actions? In other words, if all events are caused by previous actions, one's own or of others, where is the actual (i.e., "first") cause? Buddhist theology, as it turns out, is arguably incoherent because it rejects monocausality yet recognizes that events are outcomes of actions (Kalupahana 1975). It is no wonder that online, Buddhists simplify their causal inferences by appeals, however theologically incorrect, to luck.

Christian theology suffers from the same incoherence. There is a popular notion in Christian cultures that is quite similar to the notion of karma: *What goes around comes around*. As is the case with Buddhism, however, Christian theology is not so simple. Consider again the issue I raised in chapter 5 concerning divine sovereignty. Though Christianity, not to mention Judaism, Islam, and all theistic conceptual schemes, turns on the notion of divine agents, most Christians do not imagine that God controls every event in the world (and those who do must wrestle with the subsequent problem of theodicy). Interestingly, in the (1996) studies by Lupfer and colleagues, luck was given as the cause of events, both non-life-altering and life-altering (e.g., financial windfall and terminal illness), in some cases more so than God—even by theologically conservative Christians. So why don't people believe that God is in control, even when they should? Again, theologically correct postulations are often cognitively burdensome; luck attributions, as I will demonstrate, are more efficient in some cases.

The Cognitive Efficiency of Luck Representations

Why are luck attributions more efficient than theologically correct postulations? One answer already provided is that theologies are produced deductively, but the mind tends to think abductively. The reason for this is threefold. First, abductive reasoning is much faster than deductive reasoning. Second, deductive reasoning is too restrictive for online thought. Third, abductive reasoning does more broad work than deductive reasoning.

As noted, deductive reasoning involves deducing a conclusion from a set of premises according to a number of rules of inference. The rules of inference constrain the ways in which conclusions can result; they are rules of thought. A typical example of a deductive argument is a "syllogism," such as the following:

> All jocks are dumb.
> Jason Slone is a jock.
> Therefore, Jason Slone is dumb.

What's important about deductive arguments is that the truth of the conclusion is guaranteed if the premises are true and the logical deduction follows the established rules of inference. In other words, if the premise(s) is true, and the rules of inference are followed properly, then the conclusion will be true.

There are, unfortunately, significant problems with deductive thought that prevent this method of analysis from being widely used (or maybe even preferred). For one, the need for the premise to be true weakens the possibilities of the conclusion being true. What if not all jocks are dumb? Might there be one smart jock somewhere in the world? If so, then the conclusion of this syllogism is false (even though by the rules of inference it is valid).

Furthermore, consider how long it takes to deduce a conclusion about the mental prowess of Jason Slone. Not only does the syllogism require prior knowledge, in this case about jocks being dumb, but also deductions are concluded "downward" via successive stages of thought. Imagine if humans had to do this with every generated idea. We would spend most of our time processing data like mathematical calculators—although performing functions at a much, much slower rate.

Second, deductive reasoning is restrictive. What if, after all that time-consuming effort it takes to deduce conclusions from premises, the premises turn out to be wrong? To construct a different answer would require another lengthy trek through a deductive process, and there would be no guarantee that that answer would be correct either. Here's an example.

All women are good cooks.
My wife is a woman.
Therefore, my wife is a good cook.

What if it turns out that all women are not good cooks? One might try this:

All women from Minnesota are good cooks.
My wife is a woman from Minnesota.
My wife is a good cook.

What if my wife is not a good cook? One might try this:

All women from Minnesota, except my wife, are good cooks.

This statement, however, has an incoherent premise. If one woman from Minnesota is not a good cook, then the premise cannot include the pretense "all." If a premise cannot be inclusive it turns out to be very weak indeed.

The final problem is related to the last statement. Deductive reasoning involves starting from general, ideally universal, premises and deducing from those premises a conclusion to a specific problem. If the problem is, say, that my wife is a bad cook, I would have a seemingly infinite number of premises from which to begin my deductive line of thought. "All married women are bad cooks." "All adults who were raised in cold climates are bad cooks." "All college graduates are bad cooks." "All fans of reality television shows are bad cooks."

As noted earlier, most cognitive tasks require us to make rapid judgments about what's going on in our world, so that we might react appropriately to our given situations. Imagine if we had to use theologically constrained deductive reasoning. Our thinking might go something like this. "God is the creator of all life. Humans are part of life. My wife is a human. All humans must eat. My wife must eat. All humans eat cooked food. My wife eats cooked food. All cooked food must be prepared by other humans." You can see where this is going. This kind of thinking takes up too much time for our everyday traffic with the world, it is too restrictive, and it only deals with the event covered by the logical conclusion. For obvious reasons, most people don't think this way.

Abductive thought is much more efficient (though maybe not better) because cognitive tasks are typically problems to be solved with explanations. If the problem to solve is explaining why my wife is a bad cook (she's not, it's just a hypothetical case), then I can do so very quickly by inferring an answer that, if true, would explain the puzzle. In this way, abductive reasoning starts with a conclusion and skips all the steps required by deductive logic. For example, maybe my wife is a bad cook because she never learned how to do it properly. This abductive answer to the problem is plausible and if true solves the problem. If it's not true, I can quickly discard the hypothesis and generate a new one. If she had in fact learned how to cook well, maybe she can't cook well because she is under a lot of stress at work and so is distracted at home. Or maybe she is trying to make me lose weight and so is purposely cooking poorly tasting food. Or maybe I bought cheap, bad-tasting groceries for her to cook with. This list, too, is infinite in its possibilities but is more easily perused for answers (few steps required).

What is striking about this way of thinking is that so much of what is involved in generating abductive ideas is only *tacitly* known. Abductive reasoning takes for granted a whole host of assumptions that are necessary for the abductive generalization to be constructed at all. Just think of what is assumed in the foregoing inferences. In terms of ontology, we know, without having to consciously think about it, that my wife is a human and thus a psychological agent. Moreover, it assumes she intends to produce a cooked meal that tastes good (or bad, as the case may be) and the problem itself assumes that my wife is the primary cause of the food tasting bad. Then, I search for causes of that cause. Intuitively, I assume not only that there is a cause but also that I can detect it (wherever "it" may be).

This type of causal reasoning is central to cognition. Humans need to know why things happen—not just to figure out how to solve the problem of having to eat bad food, but to survive at all. The belief in luck, like the belief in religious ideas, is a by-product of the cognitive capacity to infer causes of events in the world.

Events

An important distinction to keep in mind is that happenings simply occur; events are caused (McCauley & Lawson 2002). As I have already noted, causality is a central feature of cognition, and as such causal reasoning has become an important area of research in the past few decades. What scientists have discovered is that causality is inferred from domain-specific tacit knowledge about what kinds of things are in the world and how those things work. An important piece of the puzzle, though, is that human conceptualization of causality changes over time as our cognitive capacities develop.

Early in life, human beings are deterministic in their thinking. Young children seem to have very clear ideas about how things in the world ought to work. This is revealed by studies in which infants and young children are shown events in which things happen that aren't supposed to. For example, in one study children are shown an event in which a ball goes directly through a wall (Spelke, Phillips, & Woodward 1995). Needless to say, their reactions showed an element of surprise. Given their intuitive physics, they know that this kind of event isn't supposed to happen. Sometime around the age of six or seven, however, children begin to switch from a deterministic view of the world to a probabilistic one. Children begin to infer outcomes of events based on a tacit knowledge of probability grounded in intuitive ontology. It is at this age, according to Piaget and Inhelder, that children begin to develop and hone an understanding of "chance." At this stage of development, children begin to think that event-outcomes are not a matter of either-or but of more-or-less likely to occur. Prior to this stage of development, children believe that every event outcome has a cause, even if the cause is hidden (think of why magicians are so entertaining!). Central to our ability to conceptualize probability is the capacity to represent the frequency of occurrences, and frequency concepts reveal a sense of expectation about how the world is supposed to work. The primary difference between children under and over the age of six is that in the former group, event-outcomes *must* happen in a certain way, whereas in the latter, children seem to think that event outcomes will most likely, but not necessarily, happen in a certain way (Piaget & Inhelder 1976).

Piaget and Inhelder's research suggests that humans regularly perform a kind of "informal calculus of probability" (Vyse 1997, p. 95). Humans construct probabilistic theories about why things happen as well as what kinds of things will happen. In this sense, probabilistic inferences both explain and predict. Now, were the world not to operate in recognizable patterns (either real or imagined), we would have great difficulty in making sense of why things happen, and in turn great difficulty in making and acting on predictions about how things are reasonably going to happen. So it is very useful. However, intuitive probability is not exactly like scientific probability, and so it is important to consider the differences.

Probability

Scientific probability turns on fairly precise mathematical formulae that can be tested for confirmation or disconfirmation. The goal is not perfect prediction per se but rather to arrive at the odds, or probability, that a particular outcome will occur. One of the most famous experiments in statistics that reveals the phenomena of randomness and variability is the flipping of coins. In this experiment, researchers flip one or two fair coins. There are four possible outcomes when two coins are flipped: HH (heads/heads), TT (tails/

tails), HT (heads/tails), and TH (tails/heads). Since HH is only one in four possible outcomes, the probability that a flip of the coins will result in HH is 1:4 or 25 percent. This also goes for TT. However, since there are two variations of the same result for a non-same-side up, either TH or HT produces the same result. The possible outcomes for this set are two out of four. Therefore, the probability that a flip of the coins will render a non-same-sided result is 2:4 or 50 percent. Thus, we can say that there is twice as much of a chance that two flips will result in a non-same-sided result (TH or HT) as a same-sided result (TT or HH) because probability is the number of desired outcomes divided by the number of possible outcomes.

There are no guarantees of any particular outcome in this experiment. There are only probabilities that the results will show up in such patterns. In the classical experiment that shows the reliability of this theory, subjects flip two coins, but only once or twice. In just a few flips of the coins, there does not appear to be any recognizable pattern. The results are "random." However, when the coins are flipped a hundred times a pattern emerges: around twenty-five TTs, twenty-five HHs, and fifty TH/HTs. For probability theorists, this shows that if something is done once, anything can happen. However, if something is done over and over, depending on its structural limitations, a pattern becomes visible (note that this is why this method is an effective way to determine the beginnings of games—since the results guarantee no outcomes for one side or the other, it is fair).

Importantly, each flip of the coins in this experiment is completely independent. In other words, what happens on one flip has no influence on what will result in the next flip . . . even though we "see" a pattern when many flips are involved. Despite this fact, human beings tend to believe that the consecutive flips of the coin are related in some way or another. For example, when presented with two possible sequences of flip results, research subjects have shown a preference for the likelihood of a random sequence. If asked to infer which sequence is more likely to result from random flips of coins, subjects prefer a sequence like TT, HT, TT, TH, HT, HH over something like HH, HH, HH, HH, HH, HH. Though the possibility of either sequence occurring is exactly the same, humans "know" intuitively that the latter is less likely to happen. Even more interesting, because the latter sequence does not appear to be random at all, people infer that there must be hidden forces at work causing the sequence to occur as such (Vyse 1997).

In a similar experiment designed to elicit inferences about likelihood, subjects were shown an outcome sequence that appeared to be systematically random (and thus not really random at all!). Subjects had difficulty accepting that random flips of a single coin could produce effects like H, T, H, T, H, T, H, T or H, H, T, T, H, H, T, T, even though these results are possible. These sequence results seem to violate our expectations about how randomness ought to occur (itself—how randomness ought to occur—a strange concept) (Vyse 1997, p. 100).

Having deeply rooted expectations about how the world ought to work leads to other interesting psychological effects regarding the belief in luck. Two common cognitive mistakes that humans make collectively constitute the "gambler's fallacy," which is based on the beliefs that (1) forces outside wholly mechanical processes can influence an outcome, and that (2) positive and negative results ought to average out over a period of time (also known as the "law of averages"). The first case involves the attempt to influence the outcome of entirely mechanical and random processes, for example, by performing superstitious actions. This phenomenon is known as the gambler's fallacy for good reasons; gamblers are notoriously prone to performing rituals and other actions that they think will influence the outcome of games (even games of chance). Those who play games like roulette or craps often chant incantations before their turn (e.g., "Come on sevens. Daddy needs a new pair of shoes!"). While in some sense, humans "know" that the roulette wheel is just a mechanical device and thus that the result of the game is random, anyone who has ever gambled knows how natural it feels to try to influence the outcome, often by talking to the game as if it had some kind of psychological agency.

The second aspect of the gambler's fallacy, which is widespread among people whose livelihoods (and lives in some cases) depend on variables outside of their control, like athletes, fishing boat captains, stock traders, and so on is the belief in the law of averages. Informally, this is known as someone or something being "due." In this case, in games, sporting matches, and other activities in which forces beyond one's control determine outcomes, participants come to believe that a string of bad luck will be countered by a string of good luck. Athletes believe that when they go into "slumps," they need a "break," or a "stroke of good luck," to turn things around.

On the other hand, athletes are prone to the belief in having a "hot hand" and will perform arbitrary actions that they believe will make the string of good luck continue (e.g., Wade Boggs eating chicken on every game day because he had good luck in one game early in his career after having eaten chicken) (Gilovich, Vallone, & Tversky 1985.) Gamblers also believe that a string of losses at a game of chance increases the sense that a person is about to win, despite the fact that (as was shown in the coin-flipping example) each successive try in the game occurs independently. Thus, one could quite possibly lose every single time forever, but most people would have a hard time believing this statistical possibility—and maybe for good probabilistic reasons (Becker 1975; Blackmore 1985; Cohen 1960; R. Falk 1981, 1989; Killeen 1977; Langer & Roth 1975; Lopes & Oden 1987; Oldman 1974; Timberlake & Lucas 1985).

The belief that luck "evens out" in the world is a presumption that is at the heart of not just luck beliefs but also of religious ideas about moral retribution (e.g., karma, sin, etc.). In this sense, it is less the case that religious ideas cause people to think that things even out in life. Rather, it is because human beings intuitively presume so that religious ideas like karma in Buddhism and sin in Christianity are believable (Boyer 2001).

Coincidence

In addition to the varieties of cognitive inferences humans make regarding randomness and variability, we also seem prone to spotting coincidences and to representing them as fateful events. Despite the mechanical randomness of many of life's events, humans tend to "link" events together in ways that make their relationships meaningful. Consider the popularity of James Redfield's (1993) book *The Celestine Prophecy.* The book's message was that life moves in sequences of important events that link people with their "destinies." Redfield guided readers to reflect on the most important events in their lives, namely those that have led them to where they are today. Why did you pick the college you attended? Why did you meet the person you married? Why did you decide not to go to work on September 11? And so on. According to Redfield, such events are not coincidences at all but are in fact part of each person's destiny. Thousands of readers, one can assume from the book's popularity, were captivated by this idea.

The overwhelming popularity of Redfield's book supports further anecdotal and experimental research that suggests that humans imbue things and events with "purpose." The psychologist Deborah Kelemen has dubbed this tendency "promiscuous teleology." Her research has shown that both children and adults are comfortable with representing objects and events with "reasons" for existing or happening. Rocks are pointy for a reason. Cups have handles for a reason. Even imaginary animals with strange features (invented for the study) have those strange features for a reason (Kelemen 1999a, 1999b, 1999c, 1999d). Given this tendency to want to think of things happening "for a reason," it is no wonder that creationist accounts of human origins are still more appealing for some than evolutionary theory (Evans 2001). Given a choice between thinking of humans as existing for a reason/purpose or as existing by random genetic accident, the former is obviously much more appealing to a promiscuously teleological mind.

Making inferential judgments is thus based on biased preconceptions about why events occur (for a reason), and much of this bias is based in intuitions about the likelihood of events occurring (very likely ↔ unlikely). One interesting illustration of this was produced by cognitive psychologists who asked a classroom of college students about the likelihood of two people in the same class having the same birthday. As they predicted, most students were convinced that the likelihood was very low, and therefore if two students did share the same birthday, it would be a coincidence. As it turns out, the probability is actually higher than fifty percent for classes with at least twenty-three students. This example, when tested in classrooms, has proven to shock students on numerous occasions (and as such has become a favorite tool of professors of mathematics and statistics) because it violates our expectations about the likelihood of the event occurring (Paulos 1988).

Furthermore, the element of surprise that underlies coincidence seems to lead people to infer that a hidden cause must be at play in unlikely events. It also reveals that human beings, when they infer the causes of events (including the likelihood of their occurrence), employ selective remembering, which enhances the feeling of the "specialness" of coincidental events (Vyse 1997). Consider again the case of the coincidence of shared birth dates. What's so striking about this case is that in a class of twenty-three students or more, subjects are shocked to learn that two people have the same birthday but ignore the fact that at least twenty-one students *did not* share the same birth date. This suggests that we are pattern seekers. We focus on singular events that are seemingly congruent but ignore the overwhelming majority of events that are not. This phenomenon is the basis of the notion that humans live in a "small world." Whenever we meet another person with whom we have some remote connection, we croon "What a coincidence—what a small world!" The connection seems too random to be random.

What all of this suggests is that a good portion of human thought is based not on what's learned from culture per se but rather on the intuitive inferences we naturally generate. Inferences involve various reasoning strategies, including postulations and presumptions based on tacit assumptions about the world and its workings. Humans employ inferential shortcuts to make sense of the world, and the shortcuts we use reveal that our minds bias reality in certain ways. We might justifiably count the belief in luck, and the tendency to believe one can influence luck, as shortcut thinking.

Moreover, it is interesting to note that this kind of thinking persists in our modern (i.e., scientific) world. With citizens of both the United States and countries of South Asia exposed from early on to scientific ideas about how the world works, why do people still remain "superstitious"? As is the case with the supposed influence of theology, psychologists are discovering that scientific ideas might have less effect on human beings' online thinking than we assume (or wish). Again, consider the case of the "rising" and "setting" sun. Despite the fact that we know the sun does not move around the Earth, we still represent it as if it does.

The reason that we are still inclined to prefer economical reasoning strategies like abduction is that we are biological products of evolution by natural selection. The cognitive strategies of perception, representation, and control we naturally employ are an essential feature of our genetic endowment. Obviously, in order to control what's around us, we need to grasp what's happening. However, most of our "theories" about what is going on in our world must be constructed because we operate on incomplete data. When we hear a rustling sound in the woods, we don't have all of the data we need to know what's actually happening, but we can infer that we ought to be on high alert. We presume that what is in the woods is some kind of psychological agent. We also presume that the agent has intentions, such as possibly wanting to eat us. We then infer that the likelihood of that something eating us decreases significantly if we leave the area immediately. Notice that all of these presumptions are inferred. We don't have to calculate this information deductively.

The inferential process described in this example shows just how important control is for our survival. Gaining control of a situation requires mental processes with a variety of cognitive tasks, and doing so rapidly. This process turns out to be employed for most situations in our daily lives. When humans encounter circumstances in which they appear to have no control, we shouldn't be surprised that they will try to figure out a way to gain control. Humans simply are control freaks.

The Illusion of Control

The illusion of control is based on the presumption that actions we perform can influence the outcomes of mechanical processes (Malinowski 1948). Consider the activities people perform while on airplanes, where passengers' "fates" (note the tacit assumptions about control in the term "fate") are in the hands of pilots and the mechanical workings of the plane. Consider the rituals that athletes perform in preparation for and during competition. Consider the behavior of gamblers, stock traders, sailors, fishing boat captains, and other folks whose livelihoods depend on processes that are largely beyond their control. Consider persons and their families who are confronted with the possibility of the death of a loved one. All of these people are prone to believe in the forces of luck, and to perform rituals in hopes of receiving some good luck. Often, paradoxically, people pray to the gods for a stroke of good luck.

But, you might protest, there are cases in which luck seems to actually occur. In-flight rituals work; the proof is in the pudding. Not one single plane you've been on has crashed since you've begun to tap your forehead four times successively with a red pen. Furthermore, maybe you've won the lottery by playing your lucky numbers, or you know someone else who has. Or maybe you've gotten the hot hand in sports, and "getting hot" resulted from not washing your uniform (including your undergarments). Maybe you know someone who is just plain lucky or someone else who is just plain unlucky. Isn't this enough proof that luck exists and that luck rituals work?

This argument is one of the most powerful for folks who believe, or want to believe, in luck. Yet it is a fallacy. According to the principles of science, for a hypothesis to count as a theory, it must have as a property the potential to be disconfirmed. Such theories about the proof of luck are unfalsifiable beliefs (not theories) because evidence counts only for the belief, never against it. In such cases, if evidence seems to disconfirm the hypothesis, that piece of evidence (or its accompanying theory) is simply discarded.

The tendency to evaluate evidence selectively—a common feature of religious belief—reveals what psychologists call "confirmation bias," which is based on a correlation illusion (Vyse 1997). Confirmation bias is exactly what it sounds like, the bias to see what one is looking for, or to selectively identify bits of evidence that seem only to confirm what one believes (or hopes). In astrology, for example, readers of horoscopes "see" proof of the predictions all around. But the effectiveness of astrological prophecy is its vagueness: "Something important will happen to you soon."

Confirmation bias is based on the illusion of correlation, in which an event is correlated with a postulated cause (this is also a problem in science). For instance, athletes might believe that their pregame ritual is the cause of positive outcomes of contests. Gamblers might believe that their incantations are the cause of their winning. In these cases, correlations are confused with causes, and correlation illusions fuel luck beliefs and rituals because they lead humans to link a postulated cause, most likely one they can control, to an event.

Summary

People presume that luck exists because their brains work in such a way that they are prone to such representations. The belief in luck results from cognitive strategies that people use in their everyday engagement with the world. In order to act in a complex world, humans have to have some sense of the way in which things work, namely what kinds of things cause what kinds of events. That kind of knowledge is, for humans, probabilistic (after the age of six or seven). Thus, we maintain in our daily lives deeply seated expectations about what is likely to occur and what is not. However, we know from experience that sometimes things don't happen the way we expect. Some events are unlikely but happen nevertheless.

Furthermore, we know that events have important impacts on our lives, which is why we are so concerned with making sense of the world. We know that life is full of "ups and downs." In such a world, we strive to gain as much control as possible over event outcomes, even in cases where our actual ability to control events is negligible. The desire to do so is nonetheless strong, and it surfaces in the notion that unlikely events have the hidden "cause" of luck. Once the cause of luck is postulated, we naturally feel that we can influence that cause. Luck beliefs involve a transfer (violation) of expectations about psychological causality to mechanical causality. And, like other forms of supernatural belief, such thinking is a natural by-product of human cognition.

CONCLUSION

Religion Rethought

The cognitive science of religion illuminates enigmas in the study of religion. Scholars have heeded Lawson and Mc-Cauley's (1990) plea to "rethink religion," and we are more knowledgeable as a result. We now know that cultural theories of religion are impoverished by a lack of understanding of how the mind works and thus of why humans think what they think and do what they do. Sociocultural theories of religion assume that the mind is a blank slate that learns what to think from culture. Not only is this mind-blind assumption inaccurate but also it is illogical. One of the most striking examples of why the sociocultural approach to religion is flawed is its inability to account for the phenomenon explored in this book: theological incorrectness. Were humans merely cultural sponges, we would find that each culture would be autonomous, confined, and homogeneous. Every member of a given culture would think exactly the same thing. This paradigmatic assumption doesn't fit the facts.

A better explanation for why people believe what they "shouldn't" is that people have active minds that are continuously engaged in the construction of novel thoughts and in the transformation of culturally transmitted ideas. The cultural model of religion, not to mention conventional wisdom, implies that religious people deduce their thoughts from the premises of given theological, cultural, or scientific premises, but in fact people spend most of their time thinking abductively and so use online cognitive strategies that employ tacit, noncultural knowledge about the world and its workings. Therefore, the key to understanding religion—especially "lived" religion—is to identify the aspects of cognition that constrain religious behavior.

Three very important aspects of cognition that constrain religion are intuitive ontology (what kinds of things are in the world), intuitive causality (how do those things work), and intuitive probability (how are those things likely to work). These basic cognitive capacities not only allow us to perform important functions required for survival, like analysis and prediction of environmental activity, but also produce postulations and presumptions that might be, on reflection, systematically incoherent. In this sense, theological incorrectness is a natural by-product of the cognitive tools in our mind-brains. So, what are the implications of this for the understanding, study, and teaching of comparative religion?

First, theological incorrectness is, in most cases, not only natural but also harmless. If a person is playing golf and attributes a high (i.e., bad) score to bad luck, so what? If an airline passenger feels more secure or a sailor or athlete gets prepared by performing seemingly arbitrary rituals, so what? These cases are nontoxic. Furthermore, I have shown why thinking of theological incorrectness as "sloppy thinking" is misguided. Theological incorrectness is a by-product of capacity, not necessarily effort.

Admittedly, however, all cases of theological incorrectness might not be harmless. Consider the fact that Nancy Reagan was rumored to have consulted the stars for advice on her husband's presidential policies. What if the stars had told her to drop a nuclear bomb on the U.S.S.R. and her husband had followed that advice? Or consider a gambler who, feeling "due," bets his or her life savings on a horse (worse yet, one picked by a novice). These cases don't seem to be so harmless.

So there are, arguably, problems with theological incorrectness. Yet, if one thing has become certain from this jaunt through cognition, it is that theological incorrectness is tenacious—the mind seems to think what it wants to no matter what we teach it. No matter how many times we point out that the sun does not revolve around the Earth, folks will just go on believing that they see the sun set and rise. No matter how many times we point out that the probability of two classmates sharing a birth date is better than fifty percent, people will still be surprised when it happens.

And no matter how much we teach people that God or karma is in charge of everything, they are going to go on believing that they have an internal locus of control.

One of the most important pillars of cognitive science that we would do well to keep in mind is that humans are products of evolution. This means, in short, that what we think and do is largely constrained by our genetic endowments. This means that we are governed by our design because, over time, the benefits of our cognitive capacities have outweighed their costs. Thus, regardless of what we seem to teach people, by and large human populations will follow patterns of behavior that are the result of cognitive predispositions. This does not mean that individual human behavior is "genetically predetermined." Rather, it means that we ought not be surprised that statistically significant patterns of behavior emerge in groups over time.

Further, though evolution operates according to the laws of natural selection, humans are not doomed to live their lives in competitive jungles. Recent research has shown that the "highest" form of human achievement, virtue, is also a product of evolution. As part of our human cognition, we possess an instinct toward reciprocity that allows us to form social bonds and coalitions based on trust. In contrast, we also possess "cheater detection" devices that allow us to identify people who don't play by the rules. Thus, "good behavior" is just as adaptive as selfish behavior. From this we can infer that religion doesn't necessarily cause us to be good, that is, to cooperate. Instead, religions exploit this cognitive tendency. Religions preach ethics because people are prone to "ethical" behavior, not the other way around (Atran 2002; Boyer 2001; Dawkins 1989; Ridley 1997).

One can say, therefore, that religion is not a cause of behavior per se. It does not determine how we think or act. Yet neither does it prevent us from thinking or acting in ways that we "shouldn't." Being a Muslim doesn't cause people not to commit acts of murder. Being a Christian does not cause people not to be superstitious. Being a Buddhist does not cause people not to pollute the environment. Being religious is merely one part of the complex puzzle that is human behavior. The dichotomy between nature and nurture, or determinism and free will, is ill formed. It is a false dichotomy because we have, to use Daniel Dennett's phrase, "elbow room" to act (Dennett 1984).

In light of the fact that religion is a natural by-product of cognition, which is itself part of the equipment with which humans are endowed as a result of the processes of natural selection, the study of comparative religion should include three components. First, substantive studies of religion ought to include not just theology and ethnography but also cognitive psychology. We need data that includes not just the ideal and the empirical but also the experimental. Second, our theories about religious behavior must be informed by the cognitive sciences. Human behavior has proven over and over again to be susceptible to scientific methods of inquiry, especially given the advances made in methods of evaluation by philosophers of science, and religious behavior is no exception. While religion constitutes an object of study in its own right, it is not, as scholars once claimed, *sui generis*. Religion is a human capacity.

Finally, the study of religion must be informed by an updated epistemology and philosophy of science. The study of religion must become more scientific, not less so, if it is to be comparative. This will require that students of religion become more comfortable with the function, generation, and evaluation of explanatory theories. Philosophers of science have shown that reductionism in the social sciences is actually quite different from the way religion scholars often construe it. Reductionism is quite fruitful, and, most important, reductionist theories have little effect on the richness of human experiences. Science does not "dehumanize" humanity any more than biology "reduces" human life to cellular activity (Damasio 1994; Rosenberg 1997; Wilson 1998). Studying the perception of beauty has little or no effect on the experience of beauty. I personally know how the eye receives sensory data and how the brain translates that data into images when I look at a Monet painting. And yet I still love Monet's work.

Finally, a comparative study of religion informed by the cognitive sciences would enhance the pedagogical effectiveness of instruction. For one thing, defining religion prototypically allows for a truly comparative enterprise. Students will be empowered to draw inferences about the phenomenon of religion from their own background experiences if they understand how another system is more or less like the system they know best. Second, combining data from theology, ethnography, and psychology enriches students' awareness of the various features of religion and, again, allows them to invoke personal knowledge. And finally, theoretical arguments about the cross-culturally recurrent patterns of religious thought and action are made possible when human beings are understood as being universally similar. People are naturally aware of cultural differences, especially differences between the theological doctrines of religious systems. What is needed, in contrast, is a way for people to understand what the similarities between religions are and why those similarities exist. In this way, students can engage the study of religion as they would the study of matter, cells, mind, politics, or any other object of scientific inquiry. It is through the scientific study of human behavior that the knowledge of God is best understood.

BIBLIOGRAPHY

Ahlstrom, S. E. (1972). *A Religious History of the American People.* New Haven, CT: Yale University Press.

Albanese, C. L. (1999). *America: Religions and Religion.* 3rd Ed. Belmont, CA: Wadsworth.

Allen, C., Bekoff, M., & Lauder, G. (1998). *Nature's Purposes: Analyses of Function and Design in Biology.* Cambridge, MA: MIT Press.

Andresen, J. (2001). *Religion in Mind: Cognitive Perspectives on Religious Belief, Ritual, and Experience.* Cambridge: Cambridge University Press.

Antonnen, V., & Pyysiäinen, I. (Eds.). (2002). *Cognition and Religion: Cross-disciplinary Perspectives.* London: Continuum.

Arminius, J. (1956). *Writings.* Vols. 1–3. J. Nichols & W. R. Bagnall (Trans.). Grand Rapids, MI: Baker Book House.

Asad, T. (1993). *Genealogies of Religion: Discipline and Reasons of Power in Christianity and Islam.* Baltimore: Johns Hopkins University Press.

Atran, S. (1990). *Cognitive Foundations of Natural History: Towards an Anthropology of Science.* Cambridge: Cambridge University Press.

Atran, S. (1994). Core Domains versus Scientific Theories: Evidence from Systematics and Itza-Maya Folkbiology. In L. A. Hirshfield & S. A. Gelman (Eds.), *Mapping the Mind: Domain Specificity in Cognition and Culture.* Cambridge: Cambridge University Press.

Atran, S. (1996a). From Folk Biology to Scientific Biology. In D. R. Olson & N. Torrance (Eds.), *Handbook of Education and Human Development.* Oxford: Blackwell.

Atran, S. (1996b). Modes of Thinking about Living Kinds: Science, Symbolism and Common Sense. In D. R. Olson & N. Torrance (Eds.), *Modes of Thought: Explorations in Culture and Cognition.* Cambridge: Cambridge University Press.

Atran, S. (2002). *In Gods We Trust: The Evolutionary Landscape of Religion.* New York: Oxford University Press.

Atran, S., & Sperber, D. (1991). Learning without Teaching: Its Place in Culture. In L. Tolchinsky Lansmann (Ed.), *Culture, Schooling, and Psychological Development.* Norwood, NJ: Ablex.

Augustine. (1955). *Augustine: Confessions and Enchiridion.* A. C. Outler (Trans. & Ed.). Library of Christian Classics, Vol. 7. Philadelphia: Westminster Press.

Avis, J., & Harris, P. L. (1991). Belief-Desire Reasoning among Baka Children: Evidence for a Universal Conception of Mind. *Child Development, 62,* 460–467.

Baird, R. (Ed.). (1998). *Religion in Modern India.* New Delhi: Manohar.

Barkow, J., Cosmides, L., & Tooby, J. (Eds.). (1992). *The Adapted Mind: Evolutionary Psychology and the Generation of Culture.* New York: Oxford University Press.

Barnes, M. H. (2001). *Stages of Thought: The Coevolution of Religious Thought and Science.* New York: Oxford University Press.

Baron-Cohen, S. (1995). *Mindblindness: An Essay on Autism and Theory of Mind.* Cambridge, MA: MIT Press.

Barrett, H. C. (1998, July 11) Children's Understanding of Death: An Evolutionary Approach. Paper presented at the Annual Meeting of the Human Behavior and Evolution Society, Davis, CA.

Barrett, H. C. (2001). On the Functional Origins of Essentialism. *Mind and Society, 3*(2), 1–30.

Barrett, H. C., & Behne, T. (2001). Understanding Death as the Cessation of Intentional Action: A Crosscultural Developmental Study. In *Proceedings 23rd Annual Conference of the Cognitive Science Society,* Edinburgh, Scotland.

Barrett, J. L. (1999). Theological Correctness: Cognitive Constraints and the Study of Religion. *Method and Theory in the Study of Religion, 11*(4), 325–339.

Barrett, J. L. (2000). Exploring the Naturalness of Religious Ideas. *Trends in Cognitive Science, 4,* 29–34.

Barrett, J. L. (2001). How Ordinary Cognition Informs Petitionary Prayer. *Journal of Cognition and Culture, 1,* 259–269.

Barrett, J. L., & Keil, F. C. (1996). Anthropomorphism and God Concepts: Conceptualizing a Nonnatural Entity. *Cognitive Psychology, 3,* 219–247.

Barrett, J. L., & Lawson, E. T. (2001). Ritual Intuitions: Cognitive Contributions to Judgments of Ritual Efficacy. *Journal of Cognition and Culture, 1,* 183–201.

Barrett, J. L., & Nyhof, M. A. (2001). Spreading Nonnatural Concepts: The Role of Intuitive Conceptual Structures in Memory and Transmissions of Cultural Materials. *Journal of Cognition and Culture, 1,* 69–100.

Barrett, J. L., Richert, R., & Driesenga, A. (2001). God's Beliefs versus Mother's: The Development of Nonhuman Agent Concepts. *Child Development,* 72, 50–65.

Barrett, J. L., & VanOrman, B. (1996). The Effects of Image Use in Worship on God Concepts. *Journal of Psychology and Christianity,* 15, 38–45.

Bartholomeusz, T. J. (1994). *Women under the Bo Tree: Buddhist Nuns in Sri Lanka.* New York: Cambridge University Press.

Bechert, H. (1966; 1967; 1973). *Buddhismus, Staat und Gesellschaft in den Landern des Theravada Buddhismus.* Vol. 1, Frankfurt: Metzner; Vols. 2 and 3, Wiesbaden: Otto Harrassowitz.

Bechtel, S., & Stains, L. R. (1997). *The Good Luck Book.* New York: Workman.

Bechtel, W., & Abrahamsen, A. (1991). *Connectionism and the Mind: An Introduction to Parallel Processing in Networks.* Oxford: Blackwell.

Becker, J. (1975). Superstition in Sport. *International Journal of Sport Psychology,* 6, 148–152.

Beit-Hallahmi, B., & Argyle, M. (1997). *The Psychology of Religious Behavior, Belief, and Experience.* London: Routledge.

Bell, C. (1992). *Ritual Theory, Ritual Practice.* New York: Oxford University Press.

Benavides, G. (1995). Cognitive and Ideological Aspects of Divine Anthropomorphism. *Religion,* 25, 9–22.

Berger, P. (1969). *The Sacred Canopy: Elements of a Sociological Theory of Religion.* Garden City, NY: Doubleday.

Bering, J. (2001, October 20). *The Biological Bases for Afterlife Beliefs.* Paper presented at the Annual Meeting of the Society for the Scientific Study of Religion, Columbus, OH.

Blackmore, S. (1985). Belief in the Paranormal: Probability Judgments, Illusion of Control, and the Chance of Baseline Shift. *British Journal of Psychology,* 76, 459–468.

Bloch, M. (1992). *Prey into the Hunter: The Politics of Religious Experience.* Cambridge: Cambridge University Press.

Bond, G. (1982). *The Word of the Buddha: The Tripitika and Its Interpretation in Theravada Buddhism.* Colombo, Sri Lanka: M. D. Gunasena.

Bond, G. (1988). *The Buddhist Revival in Sri Lanka: Religious Tradition, Reinterpretation and Response.* Columbia: University of South Carolina Press.

Bourdieu, P. (1993). *The Field of Cultural Production: Essays on Art and Literature.* R. Johnson (Ed.). Cambridge: Polity Press.

Boyer, P. (1990). *Tradition as Truth and Communication: A Cognitive Description of Traditional Discourse.* Cambridge: Cambridge University Press.

Boyer, P. (1993a). Cognitive Aspects of Religious Symbolism. In P. Boyer (Ed.), *Cognitive Aspects of Religious Symbolism.* Cambridge: Cambridge University Press.

Boyer, P. (1993b). Pseudonatural Kinds. In P. Boyer (Ed.), *Cognitive Aspects of Religious Symbolism*. Cambridge: Cambridge University Press.

Boyer, P. (1994). *The Naturalness of Religious Ideas: A Cognitive Theory of Religion*. Berkeley: University of California Press.

Boyer, P. (1995). Causal Understandings in Cultural Representations: Cognitive Constraints on Inferences from Cultural Input. In D. Sperber, D. Premack, & A. James-Premack (Eds.), *Causal Cognition: A Multidisciplinary*. Oxford: Oxford University Press.

Boyer, P. (1996a). Cognitive Limits to Conceptual Relativity: The Limiting-Case of Religious Categories. In J. Gumperz & S. Levinson (Eds.), *Rethinking Linguistic Relativity*. Cambridge: Cambridge: University Press.

Boyer, P. (1996b). What Makes Anthropomorphism Natural: Intuitive Ontology and Cultural Representations. *Journal of the Royal Anthropological Institute, 2*, 1–15.

Boyer, P. (1998a). Cognitive Aspects of Religious Ontologies: How Brain Processes Constrain Religious Concepts. In T. Alhback (Ed.), *Theory and Method in the Study of Religion*. Stockholm: Donner Institute.

Boyer, P. (1998b). Cognitive Tracks of Cultural Inheritance: How Evolved Intuitive Ontology Governs Cultural Transmission. *American Anthropologist, 100*, 876–889.

Boyer, P. (2000). Evolution of a Modern Mind and the Origins of Culture: Religious Concepts as a Limiting Case. In P. Carruthers & A. Chamberlain (Eds.), *Evolution and the Human Mind: Modularity, Language and Metacognition*. Cambridge: Cambridge University Press.

Boyer, P. (2001). *Religion Explained: The Evolutionary Origins of Religious Thought*. New York: Basic Books.

Boyer, P., & Walker, S. (2000). Intuitive Ontology and Cultural Input in the Acquisition of Religious Concepts. In K. S. Rosengren, C. N. Johnson, & P. L. Harris (Eds.), *Imagining the Impossible: Magical, Scientific, and Religious Thinking in Children*. Cambridge: Cambridge University Press.

Braun, W., & McCutcheon, R. (Eds.). (2000). *Guide to the Study of Religion*. New York: Cassell Books.

Brown, D. E. (1991). *Human Universals*. Philadelphia: Temple University Press.

Brown, K. O. (1992). *Holy Ground: A Study of the American Camp Meeting*. New York: Garland.

Brown, P. (1981). *The Cult of the Saints: Its Rise and Function in Latin Christianity*. Chicago: University of Chicago Press.

Buchler, J. (Ed.). (1955). *Philosophical Writings of Peirce*. New York: Dover.

Burkert, W. (1996). *Creation of the Sacred: Tracks of Biology in Early Religions*. Cambridge, MA: Harvard University Press.

Bushman, R. L. (Ed.). (1970). *The Great Awakening: Documents on the Revival of Religion, 1740–1745*. New York: Atheneum.

Butler, H. (1990). *Awash in a Sea of Faith: Christianizing the American People*. Cambridge, MA: Harvard University Press.

Calvin, J. (1936). *Institutes of the Christian Religion*. J. Allen (Trans). Philadelphia: Presbyterian Board of Christian Education.

Capps, W. H. (1995). *Religious Studies: The Making of a Discipline*. Minneapolis: Fortress.

Carey, S. (1996). Cognitive Domains as Modes of Thought. In D. R. Olson & N. Torrance (Eds.), *Modes of Thought: Explorations in Culture and Cognition*. Cambridge: Cambridge University Press.

Carse, J. (1967). *Jonathan Edwards and the Visibility of God*. New York: Scribner's.

Certeau, M. de. (1984). *The Practice of Everyday Life*. Steven Redall (Trans.). Berkeley: University of California Press.

Certeau, M. de. (1997a). *Culture in the Plural*. L. Giard (Ed.), T. Conley (Trans.). Minneapolis: University of Minnesota Press.

Certeau, M. de. (1997b). *The Capture of Speech and Other Political Writings*. L. Giard (Ed.), T. Conley (Trans.). Minneapolis: University of Minnesota Press.

Cheal, D. J. (1988). *The Gift Economy*. London: Routledge.

Chidester, D. (1996). *Savage Systems: Colonialism and Comparative Religion in Southern Africa*. Studies in Religion and Culture. Charlottesville: University Press of Virginia.

Chomsky, N. (1957). *Syntactic Structures*. The Hague: Mouton.

Chomsky, N. (1965). *Aspects of a Theory of Syntax*. Cambridge, MA: MIT Press.

Chomsky, N. (1972). *Language and Mind*. New York: Harcourt Brace Jovanovich.

Chomsky, N. (1975). *Reflections on Language*. New York: Pantheon.

Chomsky, N. (1980). *Rules and Representations*. New York: Columbia University Press.

Chomsky, N. (1986). *Knowledge of Language; Its Nature, Origin, and Use*. New York: Praeger.

Chomsky, N. (1993). *Language and Thought*. Anshen Transdisciplinary Lectureships in Art, Science, and the Philosophy of Culture, Vol. 3. Wakefield, RI: Moyer Bell.

Churchland, P. M. (1979). *Scientific Realism and the Plasticity of Mind*. Cambridge: Cambridge University Press.

Churchland, P. M. (1988). *Matter and Consciousness: A Contemporary Introduction to the Philosophy of Mind*. 2nd Ed. Cambridge, MA: MIT Press.

Churchland, P. S. (1986). *Neurophilosophy*. Cambridge, MA: MIT Press.

Clack, B. R. (1999). *Wittgenstein, Frazer, and Religion*. New York: St. Martin's Press.

Clarke, D. L. (1993). *Religion Defined and Explained*. New York: St. Martin's Press.

Cohen, J. (1960). *Chance, Skill, and Luck: The Psychology of Guessing and Gambling*. Baltimore: Penguin.

Coleman, J. W. (2001). *The New Buddhism: The Western Transformation of an Ancient Tradition*. New York: Oxford University Press.

Collins, S. (1982). *Selfless Persons: Imagery and Thought in Theravada Buddhism*. New York: Cambridge University Press.

Connerton, P. (1989). *How Societies Remember*. Themes in the Social Sciences. Cambridge: Cambridge University Press.

Connolly, P. (Ed.). (1999). *Approaches to the Study of Religion*. London: Cassell.

Corballis, M., & Lea, S. (Eds.). (1999). *The Descent of Mind: Psychological Perspectives on Hominid Evolution*. New York: Oxford University Press.

Csibra, G., & Gergely, G. (1998). The Teleological Origins of Mentalistic Action Explanations: A Developmental Hypothesis. *Developmental Science*, 1, 255–259.

Cummins, R. (1983). *The Nature of Psychological Explanation*. Cambridge, MA: Bradford Books.

Damasio, A. R. (1994). *Descartes' Error: Emotion, Reason, and the Human Brain*. New York: Putnam.

Darwin, C. R. (1859). *The Origin of Species*. London: John Murray.

Davids, T.W.R. (Trans.) (1880). *Jatakatthavannana or The Jataka Tales: Buddhist Birth Stories*. Vol. 1. London: Trubner, Ludgate Hill.

Davis, R. (1984). *Muang Metaphysics: A Study of Northern Thai Myth and Ritual*. Bangkok: Pandora Press.

Dawkins, R. (1986). *The Blind Watchmaker*. Harlow, UK: Longman.

Dawkins, R. (1989). *The Selfish Gene*. New York: Oxford University Press.

Day, T. P. (1988). *Great Tradition and Little Tradition in Theravada Buddhist Studies*. Lewiston, ME: Edwin Mellen Press.

Dennett, D. (1984). *Elbow Room: The Varieties of Free-Will Worth Wanting*. Cambridge, MA: Bradford Books.

Dennett, D. (1987). *The Intentional Stance*. Cambridge, MA: MIT Press.

Dennett, D. (1995). *Darwin's Dangerous Idea: Evolution and the Meanings of Life*. New York: Touchstone Books.

Descartes, R. (1931). *The Philosophical Works of Descartes*. E. S. Haldane & G.R.T. Ross (Trans.). Cambridge: Cambridge University Press.

Dharmasena, T. (1991). *Jewels of the Doctrine: Stories of the Saddharma Ratnavaliya*. R. Obeyesekere (Trans.). Albany: State University of New York Press.

Dirks, N., Eley, G., & Ornter, S. (Eds.). (1994). *Culture/Power/History: A Reader in Contemporary Social Theory*. Princeton, NJ: Princeton University Press.

Downey, J. (1969). *The Eighteenth-Century Pulpit: A Study of the Sermons of Butler, Berkeley, Secker, Sterne, Whitefield, and Wesley*. Oxford: Clarendon Press.

Durkheim, E. (1938). *The Rules of Sociological Method*. S. A. Solovay & J. H. Mueller (Trans.). Chicago: University of Chicago Press.

Durkheim, E. (1951). *Suicide: A Study in Sociology*. John A. Spaulding & George Simpson (Trans.), G. Simpson (Ed.). Glencoe, IL: Free Press; original French ed. 1897.

Durkheim, E. (1995). *The Elementary Forms of Religious Life*. Karen Fields (Trans.). New York: Free Press; original French ed. 1912.

Earhart, H. B. (1982). *Japanese Religion: Unity and Diversity*. 3rd Ed. Religious Life of Man Series. Belmont, CA: Wadsworth.

Earhart, H. B. (Ed.). (1993). *Religious Traditions of the World: A Journey through Africa, Mesoamerica, North America, Judaism, Christianity, Islam, Hinduism, Buddhism, China, and Japan*. San Francisco: HarperSanFrancisco.

Edwards, J. *The Works of Jonathan Edwards*. Various editors. New Haven, CT: Yale University Press.

Eliade, M. (1954a). Methodological Remarks on the Study of Religious Symbolism. In M. Eliade & J. M. Kitagawa (Eds.), *The History of Religions: Essays in Methodology*. Chicago: University of Chicago Press.

Eliade, M. (1954b). *The Myth of the Eternal Return: Or, Cosmos and History*. W. Trask (Trans.). Princeton, NJ: Princeton University Press.

Eliade, M. (1959). *The Sacred and the Profane: The Nature of Religion*. W. Trask (Trans.). San Diego: Harcourt Brace.

Eliade, M. (1960). *Myths, Dreams and Mysteries: The Encounter between Contemporary Faiths and Archaic Realities*. London: Harvill.

Eliade, M. (1963a). *Myth and Reality*. W. Trask (Trans.). New York: Harper and Row.

Eliade, M. (1963b). *Patterns in Comparative Religion*. R. Sheed (Trans.). New York: Meridian Books.

Eliade, M. (1969). *The Quest: History and Meaning in Religion*. Chicago: University of Chicago Press.

Eliade, M. (1973). Myth in the Nineteenth and Twentieth Centuries. In P. Weiner (Ed.), *Dictionary of the History of Ideas*, Vol. 3. New York: Scribner.

Eliade, M. (1974). *The Myth of the Eternal Return*. W. Trask (Trans.). Princeton, NJ: Princeton University Press.

Eliade, M. (1991). Towards a Definition of Myth. In Y. Bonnefoy (Ed.), *Mythologies*, Vol. 1. Chicago: University of Chicago Press.

Elman, J. L., Bates, E. A., Johnson, M. H., Karmiloff-Smith, A., Parisi, D., & Plunkett, K. (1996). *Rethinking Innateness: A Connectionist Perspective on Development. Neural Network Modeling and Connectionism*. Cambridge, MA: MIT Press.

Evans, E. M. (2001). Cognitive and Contextual Factors in the Emergence of Diverse Belief Systems: Creation versus Evolution. *Cognitive Psychology*, 42, 217–266.

Evans-Pritchard, E. E. (1937). *Witchcraft, Oracles, and Magic among the Azande*. Oxford: Clarendon Press.

Evans-Pritchard, E. E. (1956). *Nuer Religion*. Oxford: Clarendon Press.

Evans-Pritchard, E. E. (1965). *Theories of Primitive Religion*. Oxford: Clarendon Press.

Evans-Pritchard, E. E. (1981). *A History of Anthropological Thought*. New York: Basic Books.

Falk, N. A. (1972). *The Study of Cults, with Special Reference to the Ancient South Asian Cult of the Buddha's Relics*. Ph.D. dissertation, University of Chicago.

Falk, N. A. (1977). To Gaze on the Sacred Traces. *History of Religion*, 16(4), 281–293.

Falk, N. A. (1989). The Case of the Vanishing Nuns: The Fruits of Ambivalence in Ancient Indian Buddhism. In N. A. Falk & R. M. Gross (Eds.), *Unspoken Worlds: Women's Religious Lives*. 2nd Ed. Belmont, CA: Wadsworth.

Falk, N. A., & Gross, R. M. (Eds.). (1989) *Unspoken Worlds: Women's Religious Lives*. 2nd Ed. Belmont, CA: Wadsworth.

Falk, R. (1981). On Coincidences. *Skeptical Inquirer*, 6, 18–31.

Falk, R. (1989). Judgment of Coincidences: Mine versus Yours. *American Journal of Psychology*, 102, 477–493.

Fenton, J. Y., Hein, N., Reynolds, F. E., Miller, A. L., Nielsen, Jr., N. C., Burford, G. C., & Forman, R. K. C. (Eds.). (1993). *Religions of Asia*. 3rd Ed. New York: St. Martin's Press.

Fisher, M. P. (1991). *Living Religions*. Upper Saddle River, NJ: Prentice-Hall.

Fitzgerald, T. (1997). A Critique of "Religion" as a Crosscultural Category. *Method and Theory in the Study of Religion*, 9, 91–110.

Fitzgerald, T. (1999). *The Ideology of Religious Studies*. New York: Oxford University Press.

Flanagan, O. (1991). *The Science of the Mind*. 2nd Ed. Cambridge, MA: Bradford Books.

Fodor, J. (1983). *The Modularity of Mind: An Essay on Faculty Psychology*. Cambridge, MA: MIT Press.

Frazer, J. G. (1911–15). *The Golden Bough: A Study in Magic and Religion*. 3rd Ed. 12 Vols. London: MacMillan.

Freud, S. (1946). *Totem and Taboo*. New York: Vintage Books.

Freud, S. (1961a). *Civilization and Its Discontent*. J. Strachey (Trans.). New York: Norton.

Freud, S. (1961b). *The Future of an Illusion*. J. Strachey (Trans.) New York: Norton.

Freud, S. (1967). *Moses and Monotheism*. K. Jones (Trans.). New York: Vintage; original German ed. 1937.

Gadamer, H. G. (1996). *Truth and Method*. 2nd Rev. Ed. J. Weinsheimer & D. G. Marshall (Trans.). New York: Continuum Press.

Gallup, G. G., & Maser, J. D. (2001). Mirror, Mirror on the Wall, Who's the Most Theistic of Them All? *Journal of Cognition and Culture, 1,* 203–206.

Geertz, C. (1960). *The Religion of Java.* Chicago: University of Chicago Press.

Geertz, C. (1968). *Islam Observed: Religious Development in Morocco and Indonesia.* Chicago: University of Chicago Press.

Geertz, C. (1973). *The Interpretation of Cultures: Selected Essays.* New York: Basic Books.

Geertz, C. (1983). *Local Knowledge: Further Essays in Interpretative Anthropology.* New York: Basic Books.

Geertz, C. (2000). *Available Light: Anthropological Reflections on Philosophical Topics.* Princeton, NJ: Princeton University Press.

Gellner, E. (1992). *Postmodernism, Reason, and Religion.* London: Routledge Press.

Gelman, S. A. (1988). Development of Induction within Natural Kind and Artifact Categories. *Cognitive Psychology, 20,* 65–95.

Gelman, S. A., & Kremer, K. E. (1991). Understanding Natural cause: Children's Explanations of How Objects and Their Properties Originate. *Child Development, 62,* 396–414.

Gergely, G., & Csibra, G. (1997). Teleological Teasoning in Infancy: The Infant's Naïve Theory of Rational Action. A Reply to Premack and Premack. *Cognition, 63,* 227–233.

Gigerenzer, G., Swijtink, Z., Porter, T., Daston, L. J., Beatty, J., & Krueger, L. (1989). *The Empire of Chance: How Probability Changed Science and Everyday Life.* Cambridge: Cambridge University Press.

Gilovich, T., Vallone, R., & Tversky, A. (1985). On the Hot Hand in Basketball: On the Misperception of Random Sequences. *Cognitive Psychology, 17,* 295–314.

Gombrich, R. F. (1971). *Precept and Practice: Tradition Buddhism in the Rural Highlands of Ceylon.* Oxford: Clarendon Press.

Gombrich, R. F. (1988). *Theravada Buddhism: A Social History from Ancient Benares to Modern Colombo.* New York: Routledge.

Gombrich, R. F., & Obeyesekere, G. (1988). *Buddhism Transformed.* Princeton, NJ: Princeton University Press.

Gopnik, A., & Meltzoff, A. (1997). *Words, Thoughts, and Theories.* Cambridge, MA: MIT Press.

Gopnik, A., Meltzoff, A., & Kuhl, P. (1999). *The Scientist in the Crib: What Early Learning Tells Us about the Mind.* New York: Perennial Books.

Gopnik, A., & Wellman, H. M. (1994). The Theory Theory. In L. A. Hirschfield & S. Gelman (Eds.), *Mapping the Mind: Domain Specificity in Cognition and Culture.* Cambridge: Cambridge University Press.

Gould, J. A. (Ed.). (1995). *Classic Philosophic Questions.* 8th Ed. Englewood Cliffs, NJ: Prentice Hall.

Griffin, D. (1992). *Animal Minds*. Chicago: University of Chicago Press.

Gross, R. M. (1993). *Buddhism after Patriarchy: A Feminist History, Analysis, and Reconstruction of Buddhism*. Albany: State University of New York Press.

Gross, R. M. (1996). *Feminism and Religion: An Introduction*. Boston: Beacon Press.

Guthrie, S. (1980). A Cognitive Theory of Religion. *Current Anthropology, 21*(2), 181–203.

Guthrie, S. (1993). *Faces in the Clouds: A New Theory of Religion*. New York: Oxford University Press.

Guthrie, S. (1996). Religion: What Is It? *Journal of the Scientific Study of Religion, 35*, 412–419.

Hall, D. D. (1989). *Worlds of Wonder, Days of Judgment: Popular Belief in Early New England*. Cambridge, MA: Harvard University Press.

Harman, G. (Ed.). (1974). *On Noam Chomsky: Critical Essays*. Modern Studies in Philosophy. Garden City, NY: Anchor Press.

Harris, P. L. (2000a). On Not Falling Down to Earth: Children's Metaphysical Questions. In K. Rosengran, C. Johnson, & P. L. Harris (Eds.), *Imagining the Impossible: The Development of Magical, Scientific, and Religious Thinking in Contemporary Society*. New York: Cambridge University Press.

Harris, P. L. (2000b). *The Work of the Imagination*. Malden, MA: Blackwell.

Hayano, D. (1978). Strategies for the Management of Luck and Action in an Urban Poker Parlor. *Urban Life, 7*, 475–488.

Hempel, C. (1965). *Aspects of Scientific Explanation*. New York: Free Press.

Hick, J. (1966). *Evil and the God of Love*. New York: Harper and Row.

Hirschfeld, L. A. (1994). Is the Acquisition of Social Categories Based on Domain-Specific Competence or on Knowledge Transfer? In L. A. Hirschfield & S. Gelman (Eds.), *Mapping the Mind: Domain Specificity in Cognition and Culture*. Cambridge: Cambridge University Press.

Hirschfeld, L. A. (1996). *Race in the Making: Cognition, Culture, and the Child's Construction of Human Kinds*. Cambridge, MA: MIT Press.

Hirschfeld, L. A., & Gelman, S. (1994). *Mapping the Mind: Domain Specificity in Cognition and Culture*. Cambridge: Cambridge University Press.

Holland, D., & Quinn, N. (Eds.) (1987) *Cultural Models in Language and Thought*. Cambridge: Cambridge University Press.

Holland, J., Holyoak, K., Nisbett, R., & Thagard, P. (1986). *Induction: Processes of Inference, Learning, and Discovery*. Cambridge, MA: MIT Press.

Hondrich, T. (2002). *How Free Are You? The Determinism Problem*. 2nd Ed. New York: Oxford University Press.

Horton, R. (1993). *Patterns of Thought in Africa and the West: Essays on Magic, Religion, and Science*. Cambridge: Cambridge University Press.

Huff, T. E. (1993). *The Rise of Early Modern Science: Islam, China and the West*. Cambridge: Cambridge University Press.

Hull, D. L. (1988). *Science as a Process: An Evolutionary Account of the Social and Conceptual Development of Science*. Chicago: University of Chicago Press.

Hume, D. (1977). *Dialogues Concerning Natural Religion*. J. V. Price (Ed.). Oxford: Clarendon Press.

Humphreys, C. (1984). *A Popular Dictionary of Buddhism*. London: Curzon.

Hutchison, W. (1976). *The Modernist Impulse in American Protestantism*. Cambridge, MA: Harvard University Press.

Idinopulos, T. A., & Wilson, B. C. (Eds.). (1999). *What Is Religion? Origins, Definitions, and Explanations*. Leiden: Brill.

Idinopulos, T. A., & Wilson, B. C. (Eds.). (2001). *Reappraising Durkheim for the Study and Teaching of Religion Today*. Leiden: Brill.

Ihde, D. (1986). *Experimental Phenomenology: An Introduction*. Albany: State University of New York Press.

James, E. O. (1961). *Comparative Religion: An Introductory and Historical Study*. New York: Barnes and Noble.

James, W. (1890). *The Principles of Psychology*. New York: Holt.

James, W. (1902). *The Varieties of Religious Experience: A Study in Human Nature*. London: Longmans, Green.

Johnson, M. (1987). *The Body in the Mind*. Chicago: University of Chicago Press.

Jung, C. G. (1938). *Psychology and Religion*. New Haven: Yale University Press.

Jung, C. G. (1953–76). *The Collected Works of C. G. Jung*. H. Read, M. Fordham, G. Adler, & W. McGuire (Eds.), R. F. C. Hull (Trans.). Princeton, NJ: Princeton University Press.

Kabilsingh, C. K. (1991). *Thai Women in Buddhism*. Berkeley, CA: Parallax Press.

Kahneman, D., Slovic, P., & Tversky, A. (1982). *Judgment under Uncertainty: Heuristics and Biases*. Cambridge: Cambridge University Press.

Kalupahana, D. (1975). *Causality—The Central Philosophy of Buddhism*. Honolulu: University Press of Hawaii.

Kalupahana, D. (Ed.). (1991). *Buddhist Thought and Ritual*. New York: Paragon House.

Kant, I. (1929). *Critique of Pure Reason*. N. K. Smith (Trans.). London: Macmillan.

Karlsen, C. F. (1989). *The Devil in the Shape of a Woman: Witchcraft in Colonial New England*. New York: Vintage Books.

Keil, F. C. (1989). *Concepts, Kinds, and Cognitive Development*. Cambridge, MA: MIT Press.

Kelemen, D. (1999a). Beliefs about Purpose: On the Origins of Teleological Thought. In M. Corballis & S. Lea (Eds.), *The Descent of Mind: Psychological Perspectives on Hominid Evolution*. Oxford: Oxford University Press.

Kelemen, D. (1999b). Function, Goals and Intention: Children's Teleological Reasoning about Objects. *Trends in Cognitive Sciences*, 3, 12.

Kelemen, D. (1999c). The Scope of Teleological Thinking in Preschool Children. *Cognition*, 70, 241–272.

Kelemen, D. (1999d). Why Are Rocks Pointy? Children's Preferences for Teleological Explanations of the Natural World. *Developmental Psychology*, 35, 1440–1452.

Kelly, H. H. (1972). *Causal Schemata and the Attribution Process*. Morristown, NJ: General Learning Press.

Keyes, C., & Daniel, E. V. (Eds.). (1983). *Karma: An Anthropological Inquiry*. Berkeley: University of California Press.

Killeen, P. R. (1977). Superstition: A Matter of Bias, Not Detectability. *Science*, 199, 88–90.

Kourany, J. A. (Ed.). (1998). *Scientific Knowledge: Basic Issues in the Philosophy of Science*. 2nd Ed. Belmont, CA: Wadsworth.

Kuhn, Thomas. (1970). *The Structure of Scientific Revolutions*. 2nd Ed. Chicago: University of Chicago Press.

Kushner, H. S. (1981). *When Bad Things Happen to Good People*. New York: Avon Books.

Lakoff, G. (1987). *Women, Fire, and Dangerous Things: What Categories Reveal about the Mind*. Chicago: University of Chicago Press.

Lakoff, G., & Johnson, M. (1980). *Metaphors We Live By*. Chicago: University of Chicago Press.

Lakoff, G., & Johnson, M. (1999). *Philosophy in the Flesh: The Embodied Mind and Its Challenge to Western Thought*. New York: Basic Books.

Langer, E. J., & Roth, J. (1975). Heads I Win, Tails It's Chance: The Illusion of Control as a Function of the Sequence of Outcomes in a Purely Chance Task. *Journal of Personality and Social Psychology*, 32, 951–955.

Lawson, E. T. (1984). *Religions of Africa: Traditions in Transformation*. Religious Traditions of the World Series. New York: Harper and Row.

Lawson, E. T. (1993). Cognitive Categories, Cultural Forms, and Ritual Structures. In P. Boyer (Ed.), *Cognitive Aspects of Religious Symbolism*. Cambridge: Cambridge University Press.

Lawson, E. T. (1994). Counterintuitive Notions and the Problem of Transmission: The Relevance of Cognitive Science for the Study of History. *Historical Reflections/Reflexions Historiques*, 20, 3.

Lawson, E. T. (1996). Theory and the New Comparativism, Old and New. *Method and Theory in the Study of Religion*, 8, 31–35.

Lawson, E. T. (1999). Religious Ideas and Practices. In R. Wilson & F. C. Keil (Eds.), *MIT Encyclopedia for Cognitive Science*. Cambridge, MA: MIT Press.

Lawson, E. T. (2000). Cognition. In W. Braun & R. T. McCutcheon (Eds.) *The Guide to the Study of Religion.* New York: Cassell.

Lawson, E. T., & McCauley, R. N. (1990). *Rethinking Religion: Connecting Cognition and Culture.* New York: Cambridge University Press.

Lawson, E. T., & McCauley, R. N. (1993). Crisis of Conscience, Riddle of Identity: Making Space for a Cognitive Approach to Religious Phenomena. *Journal of the American Academy of Religion,* 61, 201–223.

Leslie, A. (1982). The Perception of Causality in Infants. *Perception,* 11, 173–186.

Lessa, W. A., & Vogt, E. Z. (Eds.) (1979). *Reader in Comparative Religion: An Anthropological Approach.* 4th Ed. New York: HarperCollins.

Levine, M. P. (1998). A Cognitive Approach to Ritual: New Method or No Method at All? *Method and Theory in the Study of Religion,* 10, 30–60.

Lévi-Strauss, C. (1962). *Totemism.* R. Needham (Trans.). Harmondsworth, UK: Penguin Press.

Lévi-Strauss, C. (1966). *The Savage Mind.* Chicago: University of Chicago Press.

Lévi-Strauss, C. (1969). *The Elementary Structures of Kinship.* J. H. Bell, R. von Sterner, & R. Needham (Trans.). Boston: Beacon Press.

Lincoln, B. (1989). *Discourse and the Construction of Society: Comparative Studies of Myth, Ritual, and Classification.* New York: Oxford University Press.

Lincoln, B. (2000). Culture. In W. Braun & R. T. McCutcheon (Eds.), *Guide to the Study of Religion.* New York: Cassell.

Ling, T. (1979). *Buddha, Marx, and God: Some Aspects of Religion in the Modern World.* 2nd Ed. New York: St. Martin's Press.

Long, C. H. (1986). *Significations: Signs, Symbols, and Images in the Interpretation of Religion.* Philadelphia: Fortress Press.

Lopes, L. L., & Oden, G. C. (1987). Distinguishing between Random and Nonrandom Events. *Journal of Experimental Psychology: Learning, Memory, and Cognition,* 13, 392–400.

Lopez, D. (Ed.). (1995a). *Buddhism in Practice.* Princeton, NJ: Princeton University Press.

Lopez, D. (Ed.). (1995b). *Curators of the Buddha: The Study of Buddhism under Colonialism.* Chicago: University of Chicago Press.

Lupfer, M. B., Brock, K. F., & DePaola, S. J. (1992). The Use of Secular and Religious Attributions to Explain Everyday Behavior. *Journal for the Scientific Study of Religion,* 31(4), 486–503.

Lupfer, M. B., DePaola, S. J., Brock, K. F., & Clement, L. (1994). Making Secular and Religious Attributions: The Availability Hypothesis Revisited. *Journal for the Scientific Study of Religion,* 33(2), 162–171.

Lupfer, M. B., Tolliver, D., & Jackson, M. (1996). Explaining Life-Altering Occurrences: A Test of the "God-of-the-Gaps" Hypothesis. *Journal for the Scientific Study of Religion,* 35(4), 379–391.

Lyotard, J. (1984). *The Postmodern Condition: A Report on Knowledge*. G. Bennington & B. Massumi (Trans.). Minneapolis: University of Minnesota Press.

Malalgoda, K. (1976). *Buddhism in Singhalese Society 1750–1900: A Study of Religious Revival and Change*. Berkeley: University of California Press.

Malinowski, B. (1948). *Magic, Science and Religion*. Garden City, NJ: Doubleday.

Malley, B. E. (1995). Explaining Order in Religious Systems. *Method and Theory in the Study of Religion*, 7, 5–22.

Malley, B. E. (1996). The Emerging Cognitive Psychology of Religion: A Review Article. *Method and Theory in the Study of Religion*, 8, 109–141.

Malley, B. E. (1997). Causal Holism in the Evolution of Religious Idea: A Reply to Pascal Boyer. *Method and Theory in the Study of Religion*, 9, 389–399.

Martin, L. (1993). The Academic Study of Religion in the United States: Historical and Theoretical Considerations. *Religo. Revue Pro Religionistiku*, 1, 73–80.

Martin, L. (1996). Introduction: The Post-Eliadean Study of Religion and the New Comparativism. The New Comparativism in the Study of Religion: A Symposium. *Method and Theory in the Study of Religion*, 8, 1–3.

Martin, L. (1997). Biology, Sociology, and the Study of Religion: Two Lectures. *Religio. Revue Pro Religionistiku*, 5, 21–35.

Martin, L. (2000a). Of Religious Syncretism, Comparative Religion and Spiritual Quests. *Method and Theory in the Study of Religion*, 12(1/2), 277–286.

Martin, L. (2000b). Secular Theory and the Academic Study of Religion. In T. Jensen & M. Rothstein (Eds.), *Secular Theories on Religion: Current Perspectives*. Copenhagen: Museum Tusculanum Press.

Martin, L. (2002). Performativity, Narrativity, and Cognition: Demythologizing the Roman Cult of Mithras. In W. Braun (Ed.), *Persuasion and Performance, Rhetoric and Reality in Early Christian Discourses*. Waterloo, ON: Wilfrid Laurier University Press.

Marty, M. (1984). *Pilgrims in Their Own Land: Five Hundred Years of Religion in America*. Boston: Little, Brown.

Marx, K., & Engels, F. (1964). *Karl Marx and Friedrich Engels on Religion*. Introduced by R. Neibuhr. New York: Shocken Books.

May, H. G., & Metzger, B. M. (Eds.) (1977). *The New Oxford Annotated Bible with the Apocrypha*. Revised Standard Version. Expanded Ed. New York: Oxford University Press.

McCauley, R. N. (1999). Bringing Ritual to Mind. In E. Winograd, R. Fivush, & W. Hirst (Eds.), *Ecological Approaches to Cognition: Essays in Honor of Ulric Neisser*. Hillsdale, NJ: Erlbaum.

McCauley, R. N. (2000a). The Naturalness of Religion and the Unnaturalness of Science. In F. Keil & R. Wilson (Eds.), *Explanation and Cognition*. Cambridge, MA: MIT Press.

McCauley, R. N. (2000b). Overcoming Barriers to a Cognitive Psychology of Religion. *Method and Theory in the Study of Religion*, 12, 141–161.

McCauley, R. N., & Lawson, E. T. (1996). Who Owns Culture? *Method and Theory in the Study of Religion*, 8, 171–190.

McCauley, R. N., & Lawson, E. T. (2002). *Bringing Ritual to Mind: Psychological Foundations of Cultural Forms*. Cambridge: Cambridge University Press.

McClellan, D. (1987). *Marxism and Religion*. New York: Harper and Row.

McCutcheon, R. T. (1997). *Manufacturing Religion: The Discourse on Sui Generis Religion and the Politics of Nostalgia*. New York: Oxford University Press.

McCutcheon, R. T. (Ed.). (1999). *The Insider/Outsider Problem in the Study of Religion: A Reader*. Controversies in the Study of Religion. Leiden: Brill.

McLoughlin, W. G. (1971). *New England Dissent, 1630–1833*. 2 Vols. Cambridge, MA: Harvard University Press.

McLoughlin, W. G. (1978). *Revivals, Awakenings, and Reform*. Chicago: University of Chicago Press.

McManners, J. (Ed.). (1993). *The Oxford History of Christianity*. Oxford: Oxford University Press.

Medin, D. (1998). Concepts and Conceptual Structure. In P. Thagard (Ed.), *Mind Readings: Introductory Selections on Cognitive Science*. Cambridge, MA: MIT Press.

Meltzoff, A. N. (1995). Understanding the Intention of Others: Reenactment of Intended Acts by Eighteen-Month-Old Children. *Developmental Psychology*, 31, 838–850.

Meyering, T. (1989). *Historical Roots of Cognitive Science: The Rise of a Cognitive Theory of Perception from Antiquity to the Nineteenth Century*. Dordrecht: Kluwer.

Minsky, M. (1985). *The Society of Mind*. New York: Simon and Schuster.

Mithen, S. (1996). *The Prehistory of the Mind: The Cognitive Origins of Art, Religion, and Science*. London: Thames and Hudson.

Morris, B. (1987). *Anthropological Studies of Religion*. Cambridge: Cambridge University Press.

Mulder, N. (1996). *Monks, Merit and Motivation: Buddhism and National Development in Thailand*. DeKalb: Northern Illinois University Center for Southeast Asian Studies.

Müller, F. (1873). *Introduction to the Science of Religion: Four Lectures Delivered at the Royal Institution with Two Essays of False Analogies, and the Philosophy of Mythology*. London: Longmans, Green.

Müller, F. (1878). *Lectures on the Origin and Growth of Religion: As Illustrated by the Religions of India*. London: Longmans, Green; reprinted in B.

Turner (Ed.), *The Early Sociology of Religion,* Vol. 2. London: Routledge, 1997.

Nattier, J. (1995). Visible and Invisible: Jan Nattier on the Politics of Representation in Buddhist America. *Tricycle,* 5, 42–49.

Neilsen, K. (1997). Naturalistic Explanations of Theistic Belief. In *Blackwell Companion to Philosophy of Religion.* New York: Blackwell.

Neisser, U. (Ed.). (1987). *Concepts and Conceptual Development.* New York: Cambridge University Press.

Nelson, C., & Grossberg, L. (Eds.). (1988). *Marxism and the Interpretation of Culture.* Urbana: University of Illinois Press.

Nisbett, R., & Ross, L. (1980). *Human Inference: Strategies and Shortcomings of Social Judgment.* Englewood Cliffs, NJ: Prentice-Hall.

Oldman, D. (1974). Chance and Skill: A Study of Roulette. *Sociology,* 8, 407–426.

Orsi, R. (1996). *Thank You St. Jude: Women's Devotion to the Patron Saint of Hopeless Causes.* New Haven, CT: Yale University Press.

Ortner, S. B. (1978). *Sherpas through Their Rituals.* Cambridge: Cambridge University Press.

Ortner, S. B. (1994). Theory in Anthropology since the Sixties. In N. Dirks, G. Eley, & S. Ortner (Eds.), *Culture/Power/History: A Reader in Contemporary Social Thought.* Princeton, NJ: Princeton University Press.

Otis, L. P., & Alcock, J. E. (1982). Factors Affecting Extraordinary Belief. *Journal of Social Psychology* 118, 77–85.

Otto, R. (1958). *The Idea of the Holy: An Inquiry into the Nonrational Factor in the Idea of the Divine and Its Relation to the Rational.* J. Harvey (Trans.). New York: Oxford University Press.

Owens, D. (1992). *Causes and Coincidences.* Cambridge Studies in Philosophy. Cambridge: Cambridge University Press.

Paden, W. (1992). *Interpreting the Sacred: Ways of Viewing Religion.* Boston: Beacon.

Paden, W. (1994). *Religious Worlds: The Comparative Study of Religion.* 2nd Ed. Boston: Beacon Press.

Pals, D. (1995). *Seven Theories of Religion.* New York: Oxford University Press.

Pargament, K. I., & Hahn, J. (1986). God and the Just World: Causal and Coping Attributions to God in Health Situations. *Journal for the Scientific Study of Religion,* 25(2), 193–207.

Paulos, J. A. (1988). *Innumeracy: Mathematical Illiteracy and Its Consequences.* New York: Hill and Wang.

Payne, R. M. (1998). *The Self and the Sacred: Conversion and Autobiography in Early American Protestantism.* Knoxville: University of Tennessee Press.

Penner, H. (1989). *Impasse and Resolutions: A Critique of the Study of Religion.* Toronto Studies in Religion, Vol. 8. New York: Lang.

Petrovich, O. (1997). Understanding of Nonnatural Causality in Children and Adults: A Case against Artificialism. *Psyche en Geloof,* 8, 151–165.

Petrovich, O. (1999). Preschool Children's Understanding of the Dichotomy between the Natural and the Artificial. *Psychological Reports,* 84, 3–27.

Piaget, J. (1926). *The Language and Thought of the Child.* New York: Humanities Press.

Piaget, J. (1932). *The Moral Judgment of the Child.* M. Gabrian (Trans.). New York: Basic Books.

Piaget, J. (1954). *The Construction of Reality in the Child.* M. Cook (Trans.). New York: Basic Books.

Piaget, J., & Inhelder, B. (1969). *The Psychology of the Child.* New York: Basic Books.

Piaget, J., & Inhelder, B. (1976). *The Origin of the Idea of Chance in Children.* L. Leake, Jr., P. Burrell, & H. D. Fishbein (Trans.). New York: Norton.

Pine, R. (1989). *Science and the Human Prospect.* Belmont, CA: Wadsworth.

Pinker, S. (1994). *The Language Instinct: How the Mind Creates Language.* New York: Morrow.

Pinker, S. (1997). *How the Mind Works.* New York: Norton.

Pinker, S. (2002). *The Blank Slate: The Modern Denial of Human Nature.* New York: Viking Penguin Press.

Plantinga, A. (1990). *God and Other Minds: A Study of the Rational Justification of Belief in God.* Reprint. Ithaca, NY: Cornell University Press.

Pojman, L. P. (2001). *Philosophy of Religion.* Mountain View, CA: Mayfield Press.

Pope, R. G. (1969). *The Half-Way Covenant: Church Membership in Puritan New England.* Princeton, NJ: Princeton University Press.

Popper, K. (1963). *Conjectures and Refutations.* New York: Harper and Row.

Popper, K. (1972). *Objective Knowledge.* Oxford: Oxford University Press.

Pratt, M. L. (1992). *Imperial Eyes: Travel Writing and Transculturation.* London: Routledge.

Prebish, C., & Tanaka, K. (Eds.). (1999). *Faces of Buddhism in America.* Berkeley: University of California Press.

Premack, D. (1990). The Infant's Theory of Self-Propelled Objects. *Cognition,* 43, 225–251.

Premack, D., & Premack, A. J. (1995). Intention as Psychological Cause. In D. Sperber, D. Premack, & A. J. Premack (Eds.), *Causal Cognition: A Multidisciplinary Debate.* New York: Oxford University Press.

Premchit, S., & Swearer, D. K. (Trans.). (1998). *The Legend of Queen Cama: Bodhiramsi's Camaddevivamsa, a Translation and Commentary.* Albany: State University of New York Press.

Preus, S. (1987). *Explaining Religion: Criticism and Theory from Bodin to Freud.* New Haven: Yale University Press.

Prothero, S. (1995). *The White Buddhist*. Bloomington: Indiana University Press.

Proudfoot, W., & Shaver, P. (1975). Attribution Theory and the Psychology of Religion. *Journal for the Scientific Study of Religion*, 14, 317–330.

Putnam, H. (1981). *Reason, Truth and History*. New York: Cambridge University Press.

Putnam, H. (1983). *Pluralism and Reason*. New York: Cambridge University Press.

Putnam, H. (1987). *The Many Faces of Realism*. LaSalle, IL: Open Court.

Pyysiäinen, I. (1999). 'God' as Ultimate Reality in Religion and in Science. *Ultimate Reality and Meaning*, 22, 106–123.

Pyysiäinen, I. (2001). *How Religion Works: Towards a New Cognitive Science of Religion*. Leiden: Brill.

Quine, W. (1953). Two Dogmas of Empiricism. In *From a Logical Point of View*. New York: Harper and Row.

Radford, E., & Radford, M. A. (1969). *Encyclopedia of Superstitions*. Westport, CT: Greenwood Press.

Rahula, W. (1959). *What the Buddha Taught*. Rev. Ed. New York: Grove Weidenfeld.

Rappaport, R. (1979). *Ecology, Meaning, and Religion*. Richmond, CA: North Atlantic Books.

Raymo, C. (1998). *Skeptics and True Believers: The Exhilarating Connection between Science and Religion*. New York: Walker.

Redfield, J. (1993). *The Celestine Prophecy: An Adventure*. New York: Warner Books.

Reynolds, F. E., & Reynolds, M. B. (1982). *Three World According to King Ruang: A Thai Buddhist Cosmology*. Berkeley: University of California Press.

Ridley, M. (1997). *The Origins of Virtue: Human Instincts and the Evolution of Cooperation*. New York: Viking Press.

Ridley, M. (1999). *Genome: The Autobiography of a Species in Twenty-Three Chapters*. New York: Perennial Books.

Robinson, R. H., & Johnson, W. L. (1982). *The Buddhist Religion: A Historical Introduction*. 3rd Ed. Belmont, CA: Wadsworth.

Rochat, P., Morgan, R., & Carpenter, M. (1997). Young Infants' Sensitivity to Movement Information Specifying Social Causality. *Cognitive Development*, 12, 441–465.

Roof, W. C., & McKinney, W. (1987). *American Mainline Religion: Its Changing Shape and Future*. New Brunswick, NJ: Rutgers University Press.

Rorty, R. (1982). *Consequences of Pragmatism*. Minneapolis: University of Minnesota Press.

Rosenberg, P. (1997). Philosophy of Social Science. In *Blackwell Companion to Philosophy of Science*. New York: Blackwell.

Rosengren, K. S., Johnson, C. N., & Harris, P. L. (2000). *Imagining the Impossible: Magical, Scientific, and Religious Thinking in Children*. Cambridge: Cambridge University Press.

Rothbaum, R., Weisz, J. R., & Snyder, S. S. (1982). Changing the World and Changing the Self: A Two-Process Model of Perceived Control. *Journal of Personality and Social Psychology*, 42, 5–37.

Rozin, P. (1976). The Evolution of Intelligence and Access to the Cognitive Unconscious. In J. M. Sprague & A. N. Epstein (Eds.), *Progress in Psychobiology and Physiological Psychology*. New York: Academic Press.

Rozin, P., Haidt, J., & McCauley, C. R. (1993). Disgust. In M. Lewis & J. M. Haviland (Eds.), *Handbook of Emotions*. New York: Guildford.

Russell, B. (1997). *Religion and Science*. Introduction by M. Ruse. New York: Oxford University Press.

Sahlins, M. (1976). *Culture and Practical Reason*. Chicago: University of Chicago Press.

Said, E. (1979). *Orientalism*. New York: Vintage Books.

Saler, B. (1993). *Conceptualizing Religion: Immanent Anthropologists, Transcendent Natives, and Unbounded Categories*. Leiden: Brill.

Schober, J. (Ed.). (1997). *Sacred Biography in the Buddhist Traditions of South and Southeast Asia*. Honolulu: University of Hawaii Press.

Schopen, G. (1997). *Bones, Stones, and Buddhist Monks: Collected Papers on the Archaeology, Epigraphy, and Texts of Monastic Buddhism in India*. Honolulu: University of Hawaii Press.

Seager, R. (1999). *Buddhism in America*. New York: Columbia University Press.

Searle, J. (1969). *Speech Acts*. Cambridge: Cambridge University Press.

Segal, R. A. (1989). *Religion and the Social Sciences: Essays on the Confrontation*. Atlanta, GA: Scholars Press.

Seligmann, K. (1968). *Magic, Supernaturalism, and Religion*. New York: Grosset and Dunlap.

Sharpe, E. (1971). *Fifty Key Words: Comparative Religion*. Richmond, VA: Knox.

Sharpe, E. (1975). *Comparative Religion: A History*. New York: Scribner's.

Sharpe, E. (1986). *Comparative Religion: A History*. 2nd Ed. La Salle, IL: Open Court; original ed. London: Duckworth, 1975.

Sharpe, E. (1987). Comparative Religion. In M. Eliade (Ed.), *The Encyclopedia of Religion*, Vol. 3. New York: Macmillan.

Shermer, M. (1997). *Why People Believe Weird Things: Pseudoscience, Superstition, and Other Confusions of Our Time*. New York: Freeman.

Siegal, M., Surian, L., Nemeroff, C. J., & Peterson, C. C. (2001). Lies, Mistakes, and Blessings: Defining and Characteristic Features in Conceptual Development. *Journal of Cognition and Culture*, 1, 232–339.

Siegler, R. (1996). *Emerging Minds: The Process of Change in Children's Thinking*. New York: Oxford University Press.

Sims, P. (1996). *Can Somebody Shout Amen! Inside the Tents and Tabernacles of American Revivalists*. Lexington: University of Kentucky Press.

Singer, A., & Singer, L. (1995). *Divine Magic: The World of the Supernatural*. London: Boxtree.

Skinner, B. F. (1953). *Science and Human Behavior*. New York: MacMillan.

Smith, E., & Medin, D. (1981). *Categories and Concepts*. Cognitive Science Series, Vol. 4. Cambridge, MA: Harvard University Press.

Smith, E., & Sloman, S. (1994). Similarity- versus Rule-Based Categorization. *Memory and Cognition, 22,* 377–386.

Smith, H. (1995). *The Illustrated Guide to World Religions: A Guide to Our Wisdom Traditions*. San Francisco: HarperCollins.

Smith, J. Z. (1978). *Map Is Not Territory: Studies in the History of Religions*. Leiden: Brill.

Smith, J. Z. (1982). *Imagining Religion: From Babylon to Jonestown*. Chicago: University of Chicago Press.

Smith, J. Z. (1987). *To Take Place: Toward Theory in Ritual*. Chicago: University of Chicago Press.

Smith, J. Z. (1990). *Drudgery Divine: On the Comparison of Early Christianities and the Religions of Late Antiquity*. Chicago: University of Chicago Press.

Smith, J. Z. (1996). A Matter of Class: Taxonomies of Religion. *Harvard Theological Review, 89,* 387–403.

Smith, J. Z. (1998). Religion, Religions, Religious. In M. Taylor (Ed.), *Critical Terms in Religious Studies*. Chicago: University of Chicago Press.

Smith, W. C. (1991). *The Meaning and End of Religion*. Minneapolis: Fortress Press.

Solomon, R. C. (1990). *The Big Questions: A Short Introduction to Philosophy*. 3rd Ed. New York: Harcourt Brace Jovanovich.

Solomon, R. C., & Higgins, K. M. (1996). *A Short History of Philosophy*. New York: Oxford University Press.

Southwold, M. (1978). Buddhism and the Definition of Religion. *Man, 13,* 362–379.

Southwold, M. (1984). *Buddhism in Life: The Anthropological Study of Religion and the Sinhalese Practice of Buddhism*. Manchester, NH: Manchester University Press.

Spelke, E. S., Phillips, A., & Woodward, A. L. (1995). Infants' Knowledge of Object Motion and Human Action. In D. Sperber, D. Premack, & A. J. Premack (Eds.), *Causal Cognition: A Multidisciplinary Debate*. New York: Oxford University Press

Sperber, D. (1975). *Rethinking Symbolism*. Alice Morton (Trans.). Cambridge: Cambridge University Press.

Sperber, D. (1994). The Modularity of Thought and the Epidemiology of Representations. In L. A. Hirschfield & S. A. Gelman (Eds.), *Mapping the Mind: Domain Specificity in Cognition and Culture*. Cambridge: Cambridge University Press.

Sperber, D. (1996). *Explaining Culture: A Naturalistic Approach*. Oxford: Blackwell.

Sperber, D., Premack, D., & Premack, A. J. (Eds.). (1995). *Causal Cognition: A Multidisciplinary Debate*. New York: Oxford University Press.

Spilka, B., & Schmidt, G. (1983). General Attribution Theory for the Psychology of Religion: The Influence of Event-Character on Attributions to God. *Journal for the Scientific Study of Religion, 22*(4), 326–339.

Spilka, B., Shaver, P., & Kirkpatrick, L. A. (1985). General Attribution Theory for the Psychology of Religion, *Journal for the Scientific Study of Religion, 24*(1), 1–118.

Spiro, M. (1966). Religion: Problems of Definition and Explanation. In M. Banton (Ed.), *Anthropological Approaches to the Study of Religion*. A.S.A. Monographs, Vol. 3. London: Tavistock.

Spiro, M. (1970). *Buddhism and Society: A Great Tradition and Its Burmese Vicissitudes*. New York: Harper and Row.

Spivak, G. C. (1994). Can the Subaltern Speak? In P. Williams & L. Chrisman (Eds.), *Colonial Discourse and Postcolonial Theory: A Reader*. New York: Columbia University Press.

Stich, S. (1983). *From Folk Psychology to Cognitive Science*. Cambridge, MA: Bradford Books.

Stout, H. S. (1986). *The New England Soul: Preaching and Religious Culture in Colonial New England*. New York: Oxford University Press.

Strong, J. S. (1992). *The Cult of Upagupta: Sanskrit Buddhism in North India and Southeast Asia*. Princeton, NJ: Princeton University Press.

Stulman, L. (1998). *Order amid Chaos: Jeremiah as Symbolic Tapestry*. Sheffield, UK: Sheffield Academic Press.

Swearer, D. (1995). *The Buddhist World of Southeast Asia*. Albany: State University of New York Press.

Tambiah, S. (1970). *Buddhism and the Spirit Cults in Northeast Thailand*. New York: Cambridge University Press.

Tambiah, S. (1976). *World Conqueror and World Renouncer: A Study of Buddhism and Polity in Thailand against a Historical Background*. New York: Cambridge University Press.

Tambiah, S. (1979). A Performative Approach to Ritual. *Proceedings of the British Academy, 65*, 119.

Tambiah, S. (1984). *Buddhist Saints of the Forest and the Cult of Amulets: A Study in Charisma, Hagiography, Sectarianism, and Millenial Buddhism*. New York: Cambridge University Press.

Tambiah, S. (1990). *Magic, Science, Religion, and the Scope of Rationality*. New York: Cambridge University Press.

Tambiah, S. (1992). *Buddhism Betrayed? Religion, Politics, and Violence in Sri Lanka*. University of Chicago Press.

Tannenbaum, N. (1995). *Who Can Compete against the World? Power-Protection and Buddhism in Shan Worldview*. Ann Arbor: University of Michigan Association for Asian Studies.

Terwiel, B. J. (1975). *Monks and Magic: An Analysis of Religious Ceremonies in Central Thailand*. London: Curzon Press.

Thagard, P. (1995). *Mind: Introduction to Cognitive Science*. Cambridge, MA: Bradford Books.

Thagard, P. (Ed.). (1998). *Mind Readings: Introductory Selections on Cognitive Science*. Cambridge, MA: Bradford Books.

Thomas, K. T. (1971). *Religion and the Decline of Magic*. New York: Scribner's.

Timberlake, W., & Lucas, G. A. (1985). The Basis of Superstitious Behavior: Chance Contingency, Stimulus Substitution, or Appetitive Behavior? *Journal of the Experimental Analysis of Behavior, 46*, 15–35.

Tooby, J., & Cosmides, L. (1992). The Psychological Foundations of Culture. In J. H. Barkow, L. Cosmides, & J. Tooby (Eds.), *The Adapted Mind: Evolutionary Psychology and the Generation of Culture*. New York: Oxford University Press.

Turner, V. (1967). *The Forest of Symbols*. Ithaca, NY: Cornell University Press.

Turner, V. (1969). *The Ritual Process: Structure and Antistructure*. Ithaca: Cornell University Press.

Tversky, A. (1977). Features of Similarity. *Psychological Review, 84*(4), 327–352.

Tversky, A., & Gati, I. (1978). Studies of Similarity. In E. Rosch & B. Lloyd (Eds.), *Cognition and Categorization*. Hillsdale, NJ: Erlbaum.

Tweed, T. (1992). *The American Encounter with Buddhism*. Bloomington: Indiana University Press.

Tylor, E. B. (1903). *Primitive Culture: Researches into the Development of Mythology, Philosophy, Religion, Language, Art, and Custom*. 4th Ed., Rev. 2 Vols. London: Murray.

Varela, F. J., Thompson, E., & Rosch, E. (1991). *The Embodied Mind: Cognitive Science and Human Experience*. Cambridge, MA: MIT Press.

Vaughn, A. T., & Bremer, F. J. (Eds.). (1977). *Puritan New England: Essays on Religion, Society, and Culture*. New York: St. Martin's Press.

Vries, J. de. (1967). *The Study of Religion: A Historical Approach*. K. W. Bolle (Trans.). New York: Harcourt, Brace and World.

Vyse, S. (1997). *Believing in Magic: The Psychology of Superstition*. New York: Oxford University Press.

Waal, F. B. M. de. (1982). *Chimpanzee Politics: Power and Sex among Apes*. London: Cape.

Waardenburg, J. (1973). *Classical Approaches to the Study of Religion*. 2 Vols. The Hague: Mouton.

Waardenburg, J. (1978). Gerardus Van der Leeuw as a Theologian and Phenomenologist. In *Reflections on the Study of Religion*. The Hague: Mouton.

Wach, J. (1944). *Sociology of Religion*. Chicago: University of Chicago Press.

Wach, J. (1951). *Types of Religious Experience: Christian and Non-Christian.* Chicago: University of Chicago Press.

Wach, J. (1958). *The Comparative Study of Religions.* J. M. Kitagawa (Ed.). New York: Columbia University Press.

Walker, S. J. (1992). Supernatural Beliefs, Natural Kinds and Conceptual Structure. *Memory and Cognition,* 20, 655–662.

Wallace, A. (1966). *Religion: An Anthropological View.* New York: Random House.

Wallace, M., Singer G., Wayner, M. J., & Cook, P. (1975). Adjunctive Behavior in Humans during Game Playing. *Physiology and Behavior,* 14, 651–654.

Ward, W. R. (1992). *The Protestant Evangelical Awakening.* Cambridge: Cambridge University Press.

Waterman, P. F. (1970). *The Story of Superstition.* New York: AMS Press.

Watson, C. W., & Ellen, R. (Eds.). (1993). *Understanding Witchcraft and Sorcery in Southeast Asia.* Honolulu: University of Hawaii Press.

Weber, M. (1958). *The Religions of India.* H. H. Gerth & D. Martindale (Trans. & Eds.). New York: Free Press.

Weber, M. (1992). *The Protestant Ethic and the Spirit of Capitalism.* Introduction by A. Giddens. T. Parsons (Trans.). London: Routledge Press.

Weber, M. (1993). *The Sociology of Religion,* Introduction by T. Parsons. E. Fischoff (Trans.). Boston: Beacon; original German ed. 1922.

Westin, D. (1999). *Psychology: Mind, Brain, and Culture.* 2nd Ed. Cambridge, MA: Harvard University Press.

Whaling, F. (Ed.). (1995). *Theory and Methods in Religious Studies: Contemporary Approaches to the Study of Religion.* Berlin: de Gruyter.

Whaling, F. (Ed.). (1999). Theological Approaches. In P. Connolly (Ed.), *Approaches to the Study of Religion.* London: Cassell.

White, P. A. (1995). *The Understanding of Causation and the Production of Action: From Infancy to Adulthood.* Essays in Developmental Psychology. Hove, UK: Erlbaum.

Whitehouse, H. (1992). Memorable Religions: Transmission, Codification, and Change in Divergent Melanesian Contexts. *Man,* 27, 777–797.

Whitehouse, H. (1995). *Inside the Cult: Religious Innovation and Transmission in Papua New Guinea.* Oxford: Clarendon Press.

Whitehouse, H. (1996a). Jungles and Computers: Neuronal Group Selection and the Epidemiology of Representations. *Journal of the Royal Anthropological Institute,* 2, 99–116.

Whitehouse, H. (1996b). Rites of Terror: Emotion, Metaphor, and Memory in Melanesian Initiation Cults. *Journal of the Royal Anthropological Institute,* 2, 703–715.

Whitehouse, H. (2000). *Arguments and Icons: The Cognitive, Social, and Historical Implications of Divergent Modes of Religiosity.* Oxford: Oxford University Press.

Whitehouse, H. (Ed.). (2001a). *The Debated Mind: Evolutionary Psychology versus Ethnography*. Oxford: Berg.

Whitehouse, H. (2001b). Transmissive Frequency, Ritual, and Exegesis. *Journal of Cognition and Culture*, 1, 167–181.

Whitehouse, H. (2002a). Modes of Religiosity: A Cognitive Explanation of the Sociopolitical Dynamics of Religion. *Method and Theory in the Study of Religion*, 14(3/4), 293–316.

Whitehouse, H. (2002b). Religious Reflexivity and Transmissive Frequency. *Social Anthropology*, 10, 91–103.

Whitehouse, H. (2004). *Modes of Religiosity: A Cognitive Theory of Religious Transmission*. Walnut Creek, CA: Alta Mira Press.

Wiebe, D. (1991). *The Irony of Theology and the Nature of Religious Thought*. Montreal: McGill–Queen's University Press.

Wiebe, D. (1992). On the Transformation of "Belief" and the Domestication of "Faith" in the Academic Study of Religion. *Method and Theory in the Study of Religion*, 4, 47–67.

Wiebe, D. (1996). Is the New Comparativism Really New? *Method and Theory in the Study of Religion*, 8, 21–29.

Wiebe, D. (1999). *The Politics of Religious Studies: The Continuing Conflict with Theology in the Academy*. New York: St. Martin's Press.

Wierzbicki, M. (1985). Reasoning Errors and Belief in the Paranormal. *Journal of Social Psychology* 125, 489–494.

Williams, P. W. (2001). *America's Religions: Traditions and Cultures*. 3rd Ed. Chicago: University of Illinois Press.

Wilson, B. (Ed.). (1970). *Rationality*. New York: Harper and Row.

Wilson, B. C. (1999). From the Lexical to the Polythetic: A Brief History of the Definition of Religion. In T. A. Idinopulos and B. C. Wilson (Eds.), *What Is Religion? Origins, Definitions, and Explanations*. Leiden: Brill.

Wilson, E. O. (1975). *Sociobiology*. Cambridge, MA: Harvard University Press.

Wilson, E. O. (1998). *Consilience: The Unity of Knowledge*. New York: Knopf.

Wittgenstein, L. (1953). *Philosophical Investigations*, G.E.M. Anscombe (Trans.). London: Blackwell.

Woolley, J. D. (2001). The Development of Beliefs about Mental-Physical Vausality in Imagination, Magic, and Religion. In K. S. Rosengren, C. N. Johnson, & P. L. Harris (Eds.), *Imagining the Impossible: The Development of Magical Scientific, and Religious Thinking in Children*. Cambridge: Cambridge University Press.

Woolley, J. D., & Phelps, K. (2001). The Development of Children's Beliefs about Prayer. *Journal of Cognition & Culture*, 1, 139–166.

Wulff, D. M. (1991). *Psychology of Religion: Classic and Contemporary Views*. New York: Wiley.

Wuthnow, R. (1988). *The Restructuring of American Religion: Society and Faith since World War II*. Princeton, NJ: Princeton University Press.

Wuthnow, R. (1998). *After Heaven: Spirituality in America since the 1950s*. Berkeley: University of California Press.

Young, L. A. (Ed.). (1997). *Rational Choice Theory and Religion: Summary and Assessment*. New York: Routledge.

INDEX